# RUTH AND ESTHER

# BELIEF

*A Theological Commentary
on the Bible*

GENERAL EDITORS

*Amy Plantinga Pauw
William C. Placher*[†]

# RUTH AND ESTHER

MARCIA Y. RIGGS

with Sheena Mayrant

© 2025 Marcia Y. Riggs

*First edition*
Published by Westminster John Knox Press
Louisville, Kentucky

25 26 27 28 29 30 31 32 33 34—10 9 8 7 6 5 4 3 2 1

All rights reserved. No part of this book may be reproduced or transmitted in any form
or by any means, electronic or mechanical, including photocopying, recording,
or by any information storage or retrieval system, without permission in writing
from the publisher. For information, address Westminster John Knox Press,
100 Witherspoon Street, Louisville, Kentucky 40202-1396.
Or contact us online at www.wjkbooks.com.

Scripture quotations are from the New Revised Standard Version of the Bible are
copyright © 1989 by the Division of Christian Education of the National Council
of the Churches of Christ in the U.S.A. and are used by permission.

Every effort has been made to determine whether texts are under copyright. If through
an oversight any copyrighted material has been used without permission, and
the publisher is notified of this, acknowledgment will be made in future printings.

*Book design by Drew Stevens*
*Cover design by Lisa Buckley*
*Cover illustration: © David Chapman Design Pics/Corbis*

### Library of Congress Cataloging-in-Publication Data

Names: Riggs, Marcia, author. | Mayrant, Sheena, author.
Title: Ruth and Esther / Marcia Y. Riggs, with Sheena Mayrant.
Description: First edition. | Louisville, Kentucky : Westminster John Knox
    Press, [2025] | Series: Belief : a theological commentary on the Bible |
    Includes bibliographical references and index. | Summary: "This
    theological commentary employs a womanist, social-ethical interpretation
    of Ruth and Esther as moral agents who overcome gendered violence with
    courage and imagination"-- Provided by publisher.
Identifiers: LCCN 2025004330 (print) | LCCN 2025004331 (ebook) | ISBN
    9780664232504 (hardback) | ISBN 9781646984206 (ebook)
Subjects: LCSH: Bible. Ruth--Commentaries. | Bible. Esther--Commentaries. |
    Gender identity in the Bible. | Violence in the Bible.
Classification: LCC BS1315.53 .R54 2025 (print) | LCC BS1315.53 (ebook) |
    DDC 222/.3507--dc23/eng/20250219
LC record available at https://lccn.loc.gov/2025004330
LC ebook record available at https://lccn.loc.gov/2025004331

Most Westminster John Knox Press books are available at special quantity discounts
when purchased in bulk by corporations, organizations, and special-interest groups.
For more information, please e-mail SpecialSales@wjkbooks.com

*This work is dedicated to the memories of
my mother, Frances Claudia Spurgeon Riggs;
my grandmother, Mamye Helen Spurgeon;
my great grandmother, Lillian Jane Beatty*

# *Contents*

| | |
|---|---|
| Publisher's Note | xi |
| Series Introduction by William C. Placher and Amy Plantinga Pauw | xiii |
| Acknowledgments | xvii |
| Introduction: Why Ruth? Why Esther? Why Now? | 1 |

## COMMENTARY

### RUTH

| | | |
|---|---|---|
| Introduction to Ruth | | 21 |
| Ruth 1 | | 26 |
| 1:1–5 | *A Family Displaced by Famine* | 26 |
| | Further Reflections: Famine | 27 |
| 1:6–18 | *Three Women in Dialogue about Their Fate* | 33 |
| | Further Reflections: Ruth's Vow | 34 |
| | Further Reflections: Hesed | 39 |
| 1:19–22 | *Naomi and Ruth Arrive in Bethlehem* | 40 |
| | Further Reflections: Identity | 41 |
| Ruth 2 | | 46 |
| 2:1–3 | *Gleaning in the Fields* | 46 |

**viii** CONTENTS

| | | |
|---|---|---|
| 2:4–17 | *Boaz's Introduction to Ruth* | 46 |
| 2:18–23 | *Encouraged to Continue Gleaning* | 47 |
| | Further Reflections: Gleaning | 48 |

**Ruth 3** 51

| 3:1–5 | *Naomi and Ruth in Partnership* | 51 |
|---|---|---|
| 3:6–15 | *Ruth's Nighttime Encounter with Boaz* | 51 |
| 3:16–18 | *An Unsettled Matter* | 52 |

**Ruth 4** 59

| 4:1–2 | *Waiting for the Next-of-Kin* | 59 |
|---|---|---|
| 4:3–6 | *Who Will Be the Redeemer?* | 59 |
| 4:7–10 | *Boaz Is Declared the Redeemer* | 59 |
| 4:11–12 | *A Prayer and Blessing for the Marriage of Boaz and Ruth* | 60 |
| | Further Reflections: Levirate Marriage and the Redemption of Land | 61 |
| 4:13–17 | *Ruth Bears a Son* | 63 |
| 4:18–22 | *The Genealogy of David* | 64 |

## ESTHER

Introduction to Esther 71

**Esther 1** 75

| 1:1–9 | *Extravagance and Excess* | 75 |
|---|---|---|
| 1:10–22 | *Male Power—Female Resistance* | 76 |
| | Further Reflections: Queen Vashti as Moral Agent | 76 |

**Esther 2** 86

| 2:1–4 | *The Search for a Queen Begins* | 86 |
|---|---|---|
| 2:5–11 | *An Unlikely Prospect for Queen* | 86 |
| 2:12–18 | *Esther Is Chosen* | 87 |

CONTENTS ix

| 2:19–23 | *A Plot against the King* | 92 |
|---|---|---|
| **Esther 3** | | 96 |
| 3:1–6 | *Roots of a Plot against the Jews* | 96 |
| 3:7–11 | *Haman Sets the Plot in Motion* | 96 |
| 3:12–15 | *A Decree to Annihilate the Jews* | 97 |
| **Esther 4** | | 100 |
| 4:1–3 | *Mordecai Laments* | 100 |
| 4:4–8 | *Esther Learns of Mordecai's Condition* | 100 |
| 4:9–17 | *Esther's Decision* | 101 |
| **Esther 5** | | 104 |
| 5:1–8 | *Esther Extends an Invitation to the King* | 104 |
| 5:9–14 | *Haman's Pride and Plot* | 104 |
| | Further Reflections: Esther as Moral Agent | 106 |
| **Esther 6** | | 112 |
| 6:1–5 | *The King Ponders How to Honor Mordecai* | 112 |
| 6:6–9 | *The Kings Takes Haman's Advice* | 112 |
| 6:10–14 | *Mordecai, Not Haman, Is Honored* | 112 |
| **Esther 7** | | 115 |
| 7:1–6 | *Esther's Petition at Last* | 115 |
| 7:7–10 | *Haman's Fate* | 115 |
| **Esther 8** | | 121 |
| 8:1–8 | *Revoking Haman's Orders* | 121 |
| 8:9–17 | *Decreeing the Great Reversal* | 121 |
| **Esther 9** | | 125 |
| 9:1–10 | *The Mass Killing of the Enemies of the Jewish People* | 125 |

| | | |
|---|---|---|
| 9:11–15 | *Queen Esther Makes an Additional Request of the King* | 125 |
| 9:16–32 | *Inauguration of the Feast of Purim* | 129 |
| Esther 10 | | 132 |
| 10:1–3 | *A Postscript* | 132 |

| | |
|---|---|
| Postscript | 133 |
| Selected Bibliography | 137 |
| Index of Scriptures | 141 |
| Index of Subjects | 143 |

# *Publisher's Note*

William C. Placher worked with Amy Plantinga Pauw as a general editor for this series until his untimely death in November 2008. Bill brought great energy and vision to the series and was instrumental in defining and articulating its distinctive approach and in securing theologians to write for it. Bill's own commentary for the series was the last thing he wrote, and Westminster John Knox Press dedicates the entire series to his memory with affection and gratitude.

William C. Placher, LaFollette Distinguished Professor in Humanities at Wabash College, spent thirty-four years as one of Wabash College's most popular teachers. A summa cum laude graduate of Wabash in 1970, he earned his master's degree in philosophy in 1974 and his PhD in 1975, both from Yale University. In 2002 the American Academy of Religion honored him with the Excellence in Teaching Award. Placher was also the author of thirteen books, including *A History of Christian Theology, The Triune God, The Domestication of Transcendence, Jesus the Savior, Narratives of a Vulnerable God,* and Unapologetic Theology. He also edited the volume *Essentials of Christian Theology,* which was named as one of 2004's most outstanding books by both *The Christian Century* and *Christianity Today* magazines.

# Series Introduction

*Belief: A Theological Commentary on the Bible* is a series from Westminster John Knox Press featuring biblical commentaries written by theologians. The writers of this series share Karl Barth's concern that, insofar as their usefulness to pastors goes, most modern commentaries are "no commentary at all, but merely the first step toward a commentary." Historical-critical approaches to Scripture rule out some readings and commend others, but such methods only begin to help theological reflection and the preaching of the Word. By themselves, they do not convey the powerful sense of God's merciful presence that calls Christians to repentance and praise; they do not bring the church fully forward in the life of discipleship. It is to such tasks that theologians are called.

For several generations, however, professional theologians in North America and Europe have not been writing commentaries on the Christian Scriptures. The specialization of professional disciplines and the expectations of theological academies about the kind of writing that theologians should do, as well as many of the directions in which contemporary theology itself has gone, have contributed to this dearth of theological commentaries. This is a relatively new phenomenon; until the last century or two, the church's great theologians also routinely saw themselves as biblical interpreters. The gap between the fields is a loss for both the church and the discipline of theology itself. By inviting forty contemporary theologians to wrestle deeply with particular texts of Scripture, the editors of this series hope not only to provide new theological resources for the church but also to encourage all theologians to pay more attention to Scripture and the life of the church in their writings.

We are grateful to the Louisville Institute, which provided funding for a consultation in June 2007. We invited theologians, pastors, and biblical scholars to join us in a conversation about what this series could contribute to the life of the church. The time was provocative, and the results were rich. Much of the series' shape owes to the insights of these skilled and faithful interpreters, who sought to describe a way to write a commentary that served the theological needs of the church and its pastors with relevance, historical accuracy, and theological depth. The passion of these participants guided us in creating this series and lives on in the volumes.

As theologians, the authors will be interested much less in the matters of form, authorship, historical setting, social context, and philology—the very issues that are often of primary concern to critical biblical scholars. Instead, this series' authors will seek to explain the theological importance of the texts for the church today, using biblical scholarship as needed for such explication but without any attempt to cover all of the topics of the usual modern biblical commentary. This thirty-six-volume series will provide passage-by-passage commentary on all the books of the Protestant biblical canon, with more extensive attention given to passages of particular theological significance.

The authors' chief dialogue will be with the church's creeds, practices, and hymns; with the history of faithful interpretation and use of the Scriptures; with the categories and concepts of theology; and with contemporary culture in both "high" and popular forms. Each volume will begin with a discussion of *why* the church needs this book and why we need it *now*, in order to ground all of the commentary in contemporary relevance. Throughout each volume, text boxes will highlight the voices of ancient and modern interpreters from the global communities of faith, and occasional essays will allow deeper reflection on the key theological concepts of these biblical books.

The authors of this commentary series are theologians of the church who embrace a variety of confessional and theological perspectives. The group of authors assembled for this series represents more diversity of race, ethnicity, and gender than most other commentary series. They approach the larger Christian tradition with a critical respect, seeking to reclaim its riches and at the same time to acknowledge its shortcomings. The authors also aim to make available to readers a wide range of contemporary theological voices from many parts of the world. While it does recover an older genre of writing, this series is not an attempt to retrieve some idealized past. These commentaries have learned from tradition, but they are most importantly commentaries for today. The authors share the conviction that their work will be more contemporary, more faithful, and more radical, to the extent that it is more biblical, honestly wrestling with the texts of the Scriptures.

William C. Placher
Amy Plantinga Pauw

# Acknowledgments

I am grateful for the bibliographic research and translations completed by Sheena Mayrant; her research enabled me to access diverse historical and contemporary biblical scholarship on the books of Ruth and Esther. Her translations informed my interpretations of the text; however, final interpretations are mine.

A special thanks to my editor Amy Pauw, who accompanied me on the long journey to complete the manuscript. She and I grappled with writing within the Belief commentary series guidelines while using my constructive ethical framework, religious ethical mediation, as a hermeneutical framework. In the end we agreed that this theological commentary is a womanist social ethical reading of Ruth and Esther.

Thank you to faculty colleagues and students at Columbia Theological Seminary, who witnessed the emergence and development of the theory of religious ethical mediation. Many thanks to Old Testament colleagues Professors Bill Brown, Christine Yoder, and Brennan Breed, who invited me to lecture on womanist hermeneutics in their classes. Also, New Testament scholar Professor Mitzi Smith's comments about an early draft helped me to clarify how I would write the commentary.

Special thanks to the Association of Theological Schools and the Henry Luce Foundation. As a Henry Luce III Fellow in Theology (2017–18), my religious ethical mediation hermeneutic emerged as part of my research project on envisioning and practicing beloved community.

# Introduction
## Why Ruth? Why Esther? Why Now?

Every day we wake up to news reports of violence—mass shootings at schools, colleges, concerts, churches, and nightclubs. Gun violence is committed by and against persons who are victimized within educational, political, penal, economic, and/or religious systems and by persons in authority.[1] Police violence and shootings are on the rise.[2] Hate crimes and hate speech have been on the rise, and the 2016 presidential campaign and the years since have made all of us fully aware of the violence of hate speech.[3] September 11, 2001, shattered the myth of the United States as an innocent nation, and many of us are now more fully conscious of the relationship between religion and violence in domestic and global terms.[4]

1. Al Jazeera, "Timeline: The Deadliest Mass Shootings in the US," https://www.aljazeera.com /news/2017/10/deadliest-mass-shootings-171002111143485.html; BBC News, "Guns in the US: The Statistics behind the Violence," January 5, 2016, https://www.bbc.com/news /world-us-canada-34996604.
2. Mapping Police Violence, https://mappingpoliceviolence.org/.
3. Conor Friedersdorf, "America's Many Divides over Free Speech," *The Atlantic*, October 9, 2017, https://www.theatlantic.com/politics/archive/2017/10/a-sneak-peek-at-new-survey -data-on-free-speech/542028/; Jessica Guynn, "'Massive Rise' in Hate Speech on Twitter during Presidential Election, *USA TODAY*, Oct. 23, 2016, https://www.usatoday.com/story /tech/news/2016/10/21/massive--rise--in--hate--speech--twitter-during-presidential -election-donald-trump/92486210/; Peter Eisler, "Hate Speech Seeps into U.S. Mainstream amid Bitter Campaign, Reuters.com, Nov. 8, 2016, https://www.reuters.com/article/us-usa -election-hatespeech-insight-idUSKBN13225X; "Hate Speech Is on the Rise Following U.S. Presidential Election, NBC Nightly News, Dec. 4, 2016, https://www.nbcnews.com/nightly -news/video/hate-speech-is-on-the-rise-following-u-s-presidential-election-824559171837; Dan Bauman, "After 2016 Election, Campus Hate Crimes Seemed to Jump. Here's What the Data Tell US," *The Chronicle of Higher Education*, February 16, 2018, https://www .chronicle.com/article/After-2016-Election-Campus/242577.
4. The September 11 Digital Archive, "Saving the Histories of September 11, 2001," http://911digitalarchive.org/; Richard T. Hughes, Myths America Lives By (Chicago: University of Illinois Press, 2004), chap. 6; Mark Jurgensmeyer, Dinah Griego, and John

I introduce this commentary by speaking about types and events of violence of which most of us are aware. But there are many forms of violence in which we participate or to which we fall victim—namely, cultural, psychological, or spiritual violence—without being fully aware of the harm being committed. Indeed, I think that we should push ourselves to consider how violence is constitutive of the social fabric of our lives—how we live complicit in the omnipresence of violence. In other words, violence is not only the events that make the news, it is also the way we daily disrespect, silence, marginalize, objectify, and fear "the Others" among us because of characteristics such as gender, race, ethnic, economic, political, or religious differences and cognitive or physical disabilities.

Both public and private, overt and covert, acts of violence are committed in the name of God—justified with religious beliefs and theopolitical ideologies. Violence can be and is religiously motivated against various groups within society as well as faith communities. Much religiously motivated violence in the twenty-first century is ascribed disproportionately to Muslims, especially by persons in the United States following September 11, 2001. However, adherents of Christianity, Judaism, Hinduism, Buddhism, and Sikhism also commit religious violence today.[5]

> To single out one religion as sole perpetrator of terror in the world would be to distort the historical record and contemporary reality, as well as to misjudge the extent and complexity of the problem.
>
> Oliver McTernan, *Violence in God's Name: Religion in an Age of Conflict* (London: DLT, 2003), ix.

There is a tendency to teach and preach about Ruth and Esther as *individuals* who are exemplars of women's friendship, familial loyalty, and sacrificial courage. The intent of this commentary is to discover how the books of Ruth and Esther help us to think about how violence is constitutive of the social fabric of life, particularly the dynamics of gendered violence. The United Nations Entity for Gender Equality and Empowerment for Women reveals that violence

---

Soboslai, *God in the Tumult of the Global Square: Religion in Global Civil Society* (Berkeley: University of California Press, 2015).

5. Mark Jurgensmeyer, *Terror in the Mind of God: The Global Rise of Religious Violence* (Berkeley: University of California Press, 2003).

against women is manifest in diverse private and public arenas of life. This violence includes domestic and intimate partner violence, human trafficking and exploitation, and psychological harassment and threats. This violences happens to women and girls at home or in school and on social media, and it intensifies when women are displaced because of environmental or economic factors.[6] The books of Ruth and Esther provide avenues for preachers, teachers, and laypersons to reflect on how religious beliefs, traditions, customs, ethnicity, and laws are among the sources used to perpetuate interpersonal, domestic, and global violence against women.[7] The social ethical reading of these books opens them up as theo-ethical resources for addressing the violence of our lives as social groups in church and society.

## Women, Violence, and the Bible

Nancy R. Bowen describes several intersections between women, violence, and the Bible. First, there are stories about the death and dismemberment of women (e.g., the Levite's concubine Judg. 19); killing or abduction of women during war (e.g., Deut. 10–14); and sexual violence against women (e.g., Tamar in 2 Sam. 13:11–14). Second, there is direct physical violence committed by women (e.g. Jael in Judg. 4:17–22). Third, there is proximate violence committed by women (e.g., Delilah's deal to deliver Samson to the Philistines, Judg. 16:4–22). Fourth, women become entangled in physical and psychological violence with one another (e.g., Hannah and Peninnah, 1 Sam. 1:6–7). Fifth, divine silence becomes an implicit justification of violence against women (e.g., Jephthah's daughter and the Levite's concubine). Sixth, God is perpetrator of metaphorical violence (e.g. Hosea 1–3).[8] What we learn from these biblical examples

6. UN Women, "Facts and Figures: Ending Violence against Women," https://www.unwomen.org/en/what-we-do/ending-violence-against-women/facts-and-figures.

7. Marie Fortune and Cindy Enger, "Violence against Women and the Role of Religion," National Resource Center on Domestic Violence, March 2005, https://vawnet.org/material/violence-against-women-and-role-religion.

8. Nancy R. Bowen, "Women, Violence, and the Bible," in *Engaging the Bible in a Gendered World*, ed. Linda Day and Carolyn Pressler (Louisville, KY: Westminster John Knox, 2006), 188–89.

of gendered violence is that violence has relational and contextual origins. In the context of patriarchy, relationships between women and men or women and women can become abusive and murderous. Women can be either objects of and/or perpetrators of violence in relationships that are interpersonal, or violence can be directed at women as social groups. In both cases, the violence is embedded in contextual dynamics and justified by cultural norms and laws. Therefore, women as moral agents must wrestle with their complicity in systems of violence (patriarchy and imperialism) as well as the way that their complicity can influence individual choices about how they engage other women individually and collectively.

Violence can thus be a lens through which we interpret texts in several ways. We can read the text asking ethical questions about how violence is used to maintain order in a racist-sexist-classist societal hierarchy as well as how women participate in liberation from that violence. Or we can read texts that justify violence as points of departure for confessing the "sins of sexism, violence, and patriarchy" while recognizing that these texts disclose how "we demonize the Other (whoever that might be)."[9]

Therefore, an equally important reading of these books is to consider Ruth's and Esther's status and choices as *members of an oppressed social gender group responding to the violence they experience in their relationships and the contexts in which they live*. Both Ruth and Esther are oppressed as women in the ways that violence happens to women—sexual objectification, legal and political constraints, economic exploitation. Likewise, Ruth and Esther are members of groups who are vilified and/or subject to persecution because of their religious and/or ethnic background; these texts might aid us as we encounter hate crimes or religiously justified violence today. The traditional emphasis on Ruth and Esther as exemplars of faithful individuals must be wedded to interpretations of these women as social actors and moral agents who subvert and resist violence against them as members of their despised social groups—Ruth as a Moabite woman, Esther as a Jewish woman. In sum, it is important to read these women's stories to shed light on "the gendered

9. Ibid., 194.

*Why Ruth? Why Esther? Why Now?*

nature of violence"; "violence is essentially an instrument of power and control which perpetuates hierarchical and patriarchal social relations."[10] The womanhood and foreignness of Ruth and Esther are keys to understanding the dynamics of gendered violence in these books.

### Relational and Contextual Contributors to Gendered Violence in Ruth and Esther

| **Sexual/Gender** |
| :---: |
| Encounter between Boaz and Ruth |
| Encounter between Esther and King Ahasuerus |
| **Social/Cultural** |
| Laws Regarding Marriage to Foreign Wives |
| Levirate Law |
| **Economic** |
| Famine; Barley Harvest |
| Wealth of King Ahasuerus |
| **Political** |
| Genealogy and Kingship |
| Male Competition for Power |

When these books are read as the basis of theological and ethical reflection upon gendered violence, these stories provide avenues for a more nuanced and comprehensive understanding of violence. Indeed we might think of the embedded dynamics of violence revealed in these stories as what I term the omnipresence of violence. The omnipresence of violence is the social-political-economic fabric of churches, civil communities, interpersonal relationships (private and public), and the geopolitics of society and the world. I contend that how to live constructively in the omnipresence of

---

10. Karimi Kinoti, "Overcoming Violence: Taking a Gender Perspective," *Ecumenical Review* 55, no. 3 (2003): 226–28. Cf. Jane Caputi, "OverKill: Why Excess and Conflict Are Both Sexy and Sacred," *Journal for the Study of Religion, Nature, and Culture* 1 no. 3 (2007): 277–92.

violence is *the religious social ethical problem* of the twenty-first century.

Ruth and Esther may provide insights about how we might respond faithfully to these issues of our time: gender oppression, immigration, nationalism, ethnocentrism, human trafficking, poverty and food insecurity, ethnic cleansing, and religious persecution, to name a few. These issues of violence are interpersonal and intercommunal as well as intercultural, geopolitical, and interreligious. Reading Ruth and Esther with diverse eyes is important for uncovering how these books can inform our theological understanding of and ethical responses to such issues today.

## *Reading with Feminist, Postcolonial, and Womanist Eyes*

Twenty-first-century readers can enlarge their interpretation of these two books by using three mid-to-late twentieth century methods of biblical interpretation: (1) feminist, (2) postcolonial, and (3) womanist. Although these methods of interpretation have distinctive features, they do share certain emphases that are often characterized as liberation hermeneutics. First, each of these methods privileges the histories, points of view, and lived experiences of marginalized/dominated/subjugated/minoritized social groups of people. Second, these methods of interpretation push readers to ask questions about how gender, economics, politics, power, culture, and religious values are at work in the text as well as how these factors inform a reader's or community of readers' interpretations. Third, these methods are concerned with discerning how faithful humans work for justice and liberation of oppressed people and all of God's creation. Although I am doing a womanist social ethical reading of these books, I will engage some other scholars who read Scripture using feminist and postcolonial liberation hermeneutics. Accordingly, brief descriptions of these two types of liberation hermeneutics follow below before I discuss womanist biblical scholarship and my womanist hermeneutics.

## Feminist Scholarship

In the introduction to *The Women's Bible Commentary*, Carol A. Newsom and Sharon H. Ringe make this point: "Contemporary feminist study of the Bible has not set out either to bring the Bible into judgment or to rescue it from its critics."[11] Old Testament scholar Kathleen O'Connor says that feminist biblical scholarship begins when women read the Bible with feminist consciousness. Feminist consciousness is "an awareness of women's subordination as unnatural, wrong, and largely determined by society rather than written into our bodies by biology alone."[12] Reading with feminist consciousness is thus the point of departure for feminist hermeneutics.

Feminist hermeneutics is interpretation of the Bible that is characterized by (1) suspicion about the usefulness of the Scriptures for women's empowerment and (2) the discovery of new meaning in biblical texts when read from the perspectives of women's experiences. Early feminist interpretation included a variety of approaches that highlighted (a) stories about women as role models of faith, (b) themes of liberation in Scripture that apply to women and all people, and (c) reconstruction of the history of biblical women within their own context. Further development of feminist biblical interpretation has exposed stories of violence against women found in the Bible and the way that Scripture is used to teach sexism and support misogyny. This scholarship also engages the question of how the Bible functions authoritatively for women.[13] Finally, feminist biblical interpretation exposes the complexity of how the Bible can be oppressive and liberating for women. By exposing social, cultural, political, and economic dynamics of gender oppression within biblical texts and the contexts from which they emerge, feminist biblical scholars are contributing to the larger movement to liberate women in church and society.

---

11. Carol A. Newsom and Sharon H. Ringe, eds., *Women's Bible Commentary*, expanded edition (Louisville, KY: Westminster John Knox, 1998), xxi.

12. Kathleen O'Connor, "The Feminist Movement Meets the Old Testament: One Woman's Perspective," in *Engaging the Bible in a Gendered World*, ed. Linda Day and Carolyn Pressler (Louisville, KY: Westminster John Knox, 2006), 11.

13. Ibid., 12–15.

## Postcolonial Scholarship

Postcolonial scholarship is concerned with deconstructing the Western history of colonizing peoples and discourses. Postcolonial biblical scholar R. S. Sugirtharajah states, "Like historical criticism, postcolonialism is committed to a close and critical reading of the text. But there are crucial differences." The following chart highlights three differences:

### Differences between Historical Criticism and Postcolonial Criticism

| HISTORICAL CRITICISM | POSTCOLONIAL CRITICISM |
| --- | --- |
| Concentrating more on the history, theology, and religious world of the text | Concentrating more on the politics, culture, and economics of the colonial milieu out of which the text emerged |
| Revealing the kingdom of God and its implications for the world | Unveiling biblical and modern empires and their impact |
| Posing questions to the text that are driven by Reformation and Enlightenment agendas | Posing questions to the text that are not necessarily motivated by a European ecclesiastical or intellectual agenda |

Summarily, Sugirtharajah asserts this: "Essentially, postcolonial biblical criticism is about exploring who is entitled to tell stories and who has the authority to interpret them."[14]

The postcolonial scholar's aim is to deconstruct Western imperialism as a complex relationship between the colonizer and the

---

14. R. S. Sugirtharajah, *Exploring Postcolonial Biblical Criticism: History, Method, and Practice* (Wiley-Blackwell, 2012), loc. 32–42, Kindle

*Why Ruth? Why Esther? Why Now?*

colonized in the past and the present. Thus, another reason for post-colonial biblical criticism is to expose the role of the Bible in Christian mission and colonization. "Christian mission has been part of the colonial project of destroying people's culture and self-esteem and associating God with gold, glory, sexism, and racism."[15]

Musa W. Dube, an African postcolonial feminist biblical scholar, in *Postcolonial Feminist Interpretation of the Bible*, maintains that there are several interconnections, land, race, power, and gender, that undergird Western imperialism in the African context. The relationship between Western imperialism, colonialism, and the Bible is the connection that is exposed and examined by postcolonial biblical scholarship. "To read the Bible as postcolonial subjects, therefore, is to participate in the long, uncompleted struggle for liberation of [African] countries and to seek liberating ways of interdependence.[16] Furthermore, Dube asserts that postcolonial interpretation of gender reveals a story of imperialism in which white males versus the Africans either subsumes women in or erases them from that story; women in colonized spaces suffer colonial oppression as well as the oppression imposed on them by two patriarchal systems.[17] Dube therefore challenges Western biblical feminist interpreters when they privilege white Western experiences of gender oppression, thus reproducing imperial strategies of subjugation.[18]

Postcolonial feminist biblical interpreters also bring their own cultural stories and religious practices to the task of interpretation.[19] Kwok Pui-lan, an Asian postcolonial feminist theologian, affirms overlapping and interwoven historical, dialogical, and diasporic motifs in a postcolonial imagination as her method for doing postcolonial reading of texts.[20] In *Other Ways of Reading: African Women and the Bible*, Dube points to methods of reading texts consistent

---

15. Letty M. Russell, "Cultural Hermeneutics: A Postcolonial Look at Mission," *Journal of Feminist Studies in Religion* 20, no. 1 (Spring 2004): 29, http://www.jstor.org/stable /25002488.
16. Musa W. Dube, *Postcolonial Feminist Interpretation of the Bible* (Saint Louis: Chalice, 2000), 19–20.
17. Ibid., 20.
18. Ibid., chap 2.
19. Musa W. Dube, ed., *Other Ways of Reading: African Women and the Bible* (Atlanta: Society of Biblical Literature, 2001), 1–10.
20. Kwok, Pui-lan, *Postcolonial Imagination and Feminist Theology* (Louisville, KY: Westminster John Knox, 2005), 29–51.

with the African cultural practices of storytelling and divination. For example, divination is an ancient means of interpretation, and Dube thinks that the assumptions and skills of this practice can be used to read Scripture and social realities for the benefit of women's thriving and justice in the world.[21] In sum, postcolonial interpreters deconstruct Western biblical interpretation as normative for Christians around the globe as they expose the white colonial worldview in all its dimensions—economic, geographic, cultural, social, gendered.

### *Womanist Scholarship*

Womanist refers to a term coined by African American writer Alice Walker. Walker says that a womanist is "a black feminist or feminist of color"; she offers a four-part definition of womanist that affirms the particular woman-centered and woman-identified experiences and contexts of African American women's lived experiences: cultural, historical, political and religious/spiritual.[22] Womanist ethicist Katie Cannon sums up why African American women religious scholars who identify their scholarship as womanist do so: "Our objective is to use Walker's four-part definition as a critical methodological framework for challenging inherited traditions for their collusion with androcentric patriarchy as well as a catalyst in overcoming oppressive situations through revolutionary acts of rebellion."[23] Exposing the interacting dynamics of race-gender-class oppression in church and society is the focus of womanist analysis, and womanists then integrate that analysis into theology, ethics, and a variety of other disciplines (e.g., religious education, psychology of religion, sociology of religion, etc.).

Womanist biblical interpretation thus has liberation from race-gender-class oppression as an earmark of its hermeneutics of liberation. In the introduction to *Womanist Interpretations of the Bible: Expanding the Discourse*, Gay L. Byron and Vanessa Lovelace describe womanist biblical scholarship as "using gender criticism,

---

21. Dube, *Other Ways of Reading*, 2–4.
22. Alice Walker, *In Search of Our Mothers' Gardens: Womanist Prose* (San Diego: Harcourt Brace Jovanovich, 1983), xi–xii.
23. Katie G. Cannon, *Katie's Canon: Womanism and the Soul of the Black Community* (New York: Continuum, 1995), 23.

*Why Ruth? Why Esther? Why Now?*

critical race theory, and other theories and methods dealing with the interlocking oppressions of black women."[24] Biblical scholars such as Renita J. Weems, Clarice Martin, Cheryl B. Anderson, and Wil Gafney offer ways to do womanist biblical hermeneutics that challenge (1) the text itself, (2) the ways that the texts have been read, and (3) exclusive principles of interpretation as well as practices of translation.[25]

Moreover, Byron and Lovelace note that biblical scholars and scholars in a range of disciplines have contributed to womanist interpretations of the Bible. This theological commentary is written by a womanist Christian ethicist who has developed an ethical theory and practice (religious ethical mediation) that I am using as the basis for a womanist religious ethical hermeneutics. Three womanist scholars—Renita Weems, an Old Testament scholar; Delores Williams, a theologian; and Mitzi Smith, a New Testament scholar— provide insights that inform my hermeneutics.

Renita Weems, a womanist African American Old Testament biblical scholar, describes womanist biblical hermeneutics as "re-reading for liberation."[26] In Weems' words: "An important part of womanist biblical criticism involves empowering readers to judge biblical texts, to not hesitate to read against the grain of a text if needed, and to be ready to take a stand against those texts whose worldview runs counter to one's own vision of God's liberation activity in the world."[27]

Furthermore, Weems asserts that it is the community of readers with whom African American women identify as they read the text that influences how they interpret it. For example, Christian African

24. Gay L. Byron and Vanessa Lovelace, eds., *Womanist Interpretations of the Bible: Expanding the Discourse* (Atlanta: SBL Press, 2016), 1.

25. Renita J. Weems, *Battered Love: Marriage, Sex, and Violence in the Hebrew Prophets* (Minneapolis: Fortress, 1995); Clarice J. Martin, "Womanist Interpretations of the New Testament: The Quest for Holistic and Inclusive Translation and Interpretation," *Journal of Feminist Studies in Religion* 6, no. 2, 41–61; Cheryl B. Anderson, *Ancient Laws and Contemporary Controversies: The Need for Inclusive Biblical Interpretation* (New York: Oxford University Press, 2009); Wilda C. Gafney, "Translation Matters: A Fem/Womanist Exploration of Translation Theory and Practice for Proclamation in Worship," 2019, https://www.sbl-site.org/assets/pdfs/gafney.pdf.

26. Renita J. Weems, "Re-Reading for Liberation: African American Women and the Bible," in *Womanist Theological Ethics: A Reader*, ed. Katie Geneva Cannon, Emilie M. Townes, and Angela D. Sims (Louisville, KY: Westminster John Knox, 2011), 51.

27. Ibid., 61.

American women belong to at least four communities of readers: American/Western, African American, female, and Christian. For example, depending on the community of readers, she may read the story of Ruth with these different foci: Ruth the woman, Ruth the foreigner, Ruth the unelected woman, Ruth the displaced widow, or Ruth the ancestress of King David.[28] From Weems, my womanist hermeneutics takes seriously the need to reread the stories of Ruth and Esther with my community of readers, Black Christian women, who grew up in the Black church and were taught that Ruth and Esther are biblical role models for how to be loyal and sacrificial for the sake of the needs of others, especially Black men and the Black community. Black women who are loyal and sacrificial are considered the "StrongBlack (sic) Woman."[29] According to womanist pastoral theologian and psychiatrist Chanequa Walker-Barnes, "For the StrongBlack Woman strength, however, takes on a particular connotation that has dangerous consequences. Specifically, strength is intrinsically linked to suffering, that is, the capacity to withstand suffering without complaint."[30] Ruth and Esther are exemplars of the StrongBlack woman, and this reading of the texts discloses how they are much more than that.

Womanist theologian Delores Williams articulates a womanist hermeneutic of biblical interpretation that derives from the biblical story of Hagar, the Egyptian slave-girl. Williams rereads the story of Hagar (Gen 16:1–16; 21:9–21) and emphasizes God's response to Hagar in the wilderness. From her rereading of Hagar's story, the wilderness experience is the site of God's response to the oppressed. God responds with resources for survival, and human initiative is critical to that survival. Williams concludes that "the female-centered tradition of African American biblical appropriation could be named the *survival/quality of life* of African American biblical appropriation."[31] Also, Williams opens up issues from Hagar's story

28. Renita J. Weems, "Reading Her Way through the Struggle: African American Women and the Bible," in *Stony the Road We Trod: African American Biblical Interpretation* ed. Cain Hope Felder (Minneapolis: Fortress, 1991), 57–77.

29. Chanequa Walker-Barnes, *Too Heavy a Yoke: Black Women and the Burden of Strength* (Eugene, OR: Cascade Books, 2014), 2.

30. Ibid., 21.

31. Delores S. Williams, *Sisters in the Wilderness: The Challenge of Womanist God-Talk* (Maryknoll, NY: Orbis Books, 1993), 6.

that are of significance to Black women and the African American community: "the predicament of motherhood; the character of surrogacy; the problem of ethnicity; and the meaning and significance of wilderness experience for women and for the community."[32]

Guided by a survival/quality of life hermeneutic the reader/interpreter of Scripture is pushed to ask questions about the responsibility of oppressed individuals and their community for their survival on the way to liberation. God is not only a God of liberation. God is a provider of resources for survival on the way to liberation. From this hermeneutic proposed by Williams and reading the text through the religious ethical mediation lens, Ruth and Esther's choices are about survival and quality of life. Ruth makes a choice to remain with her mother-in-law as her choice for survival; she trusts her instinct for survival even though the history between her people and Naomi's people belie such a choice. Esther chooses when and how to enact her power as queen in the interest of survival for herself and her community even as Mordecai seeks to direct her actions. These choices are made in the space between deception (fear of the unknown for Ruth and loss of her life for Esther) and moral courage (trusting their instincts for survival) and are ethically responsive to their understanding of what is required in the context. Even when someone else in Ruth's case (Naomi) or Esther's case (Mordecai) tells them what should be done, they do not simply do what others requested or expected.

New Testament scholar Mitzi J. Smith describes womanist biblical scholarship thus: "As a political act, womanist biblical interpretation seeks to critically engage, expose, and/or dismantle the interconnected oppressions found in biblical texts, contexts, and interpretations."[33] Smith notes that oppressive systems are violent, and African American women and other women of color cannot be silent in the face of such violence. Moreover, she connects an imperative to speak out against violence to God's justice for those who are oppressed. In her words, "If we love God, we love what God loves;

---

32. Ibid., 8 and chap. 1.
33. Mitzi J. Smith, "Womanism, Intersectionality, and Biblical Justice," *Mutuality*, June 5, 2016, 9, https://www.cbeinternational.org/resource/womanism-intersectionality-and-biblical-justice/.

we develop a passion for what God is passionate about. God is passionate about justice."[34] God's justice is the comprehensive framework for womanist religious ethical mediation hermeneutics. Just as there is the omnipresence of violence, there is the omnipresence of God's justice. It is Ruth and Esther as moral agents who become the counterforce of the omnipresence of God's justice.

In brief, this commentary is critical and constructive engagement with feminist, postcolonial, and womanist scholarship on the books of Ruth and Esther. Feminist, postcolonial, and womanist scholars are primary partners in an interpretative dialogue with my womanist hermeneutics of religious ethical mediation. Consequently, the following broad questions come to the fore: Who are the Ruths and Esthers (individuals and social groups) in our community and society, and how do they survive? What quality of life follows from their choices for survival? How are we in our communities and societies complicit in demonizing these individuals and groups of women because of their choices? What do these books say to the twenty-first century church about how to be in solidarity with marginalized people in our communities, society, and around the globe? What insights for the twenty-first-century church can we gain from these books about transformative reconciliation amid interreligious and intercultural conflicts? How can the church be a place of dialogue and intercultural encounter where we are all transformative reconcilers who are seeking what God's justice requires?

The books of Ruth and Esther invite theological and ethical reflection on our complicity in and/or resistance to dynamics of gendered violence. Ruth and Esther must make decisions that are contrary to customs and tradition regarding the place of women in their societies.[35] Also, although each woman is at risk because of the religious and ethnic identity of their social groups, she is not complacent; instead, she embraces her agency and contributes fully to the outcomes of the dilemmas in the books. Importantly, the books of Ruth and Esther push us to think anew theologically and ethically about how (1) women must survive and thrive on their terms

---

34. Ibid., 11.
35. Patricia K. Tull, *Esther and Ruth* (Louisville, KY: Westminster John Knox, 2003), loc. 120, Kindle.

in the context of gendered violence and (2) all of us must learn to live faithfully with one another and different "Others" in the omnipresence of violence.

## A Womanist Religious Ethical Interpretative Framework

### Womanist Hermeneutical Presuppositions

The womanist hermeneutics used in this commentary is a mediating ethical interpretative process that has these presuppositions:

1. The authority of Scripture derives from its power to evoke from the reader/interpreter responses that reorient her or him. In other words, the authority of Scripture derives from its power to transform the reader/interpreter's way of being and doing in the world.
2. Reading/interpreting Scriptures can nurture a person's and/or community's capacity for moral agency that diminishes complicity with and participation in oppressive systems and relationships.
3. This womanist ethical interpretative process means engaging the Bible as a source for theological-ethical reflection whereby readers acknowledge that they are mediating descriptions of reality presented in Scripture with their own experiences of lived reality in the past and in the present.

More specifically, Ruth and Esther are being read using a womanist hermeneutics of religious ethical mediation. Reading through this hermeneutical lens helps the reader to expose the way that God is perceived to oversee the world (religious) is interrelated with values and ideals about who the characters in the text are and how they live in the world (ethical). Readers (interpreters) thus ask questions about how characters in the text respond to tensions (mediate) between differing perceptions of God, values, and/or ideals in ways that transform destructive energies of conflict (violence) and redirect them into constructive energies of reconciling (mediating) ethical response. In this interpretative framework, the context is perceived as synchronous cultures of deception and moral courage. There are values, ideals, and actions that sustain these cultures and prescribe behavior. Moral agency as a religious ethical mediator happens in the overlap of the cultures (see fig. 1).

### A WOMANIST HERMENEUTICS OF RELIGIOUS ETHICAL MEDIATION
©2016

Religious ethical mediation is transformative mediation. Interpreting through the lens of religious ethical mediation means that readers acknowledge Ruth and Esther as moral agents who are practicing transformative mediation and moral imagination. Transformative mediation emphasizes conflict as a relational, dialogic interaction, and mediation is a process that promotes moral growth by bridging differences.[36] Moral imagination is: "The capacity to imagine something rooted in the challenges of the real world yet capable of giving birth to that which does not yet exist."[37] Overall, this commentary interprets Ruth and Esther as social actors who are moral agents engaging in transformative mediation in response to gendered

---

36. Robert A. Baruch Bush and Joseph P. Folger, *The Promise of Mediation: The Transformative Approach to Conflict* (San Francisco: Jossey-Bass, 2005), chap. 2.

37. John Paul Lederach, *Moral Imagination: The Art and Soul of Building Peace* (New York: Oxford University Press, 2005), ix.

*Why Ruth? Why Esther? Why Now?* **17**

violence in its varied forms in their context (from demonizing, objectifying, imposing restrictions and limitations, and physical harm that destroys individuals, relationships, and communities). In turn, these books may help us to reflect on how we might practice reconciliation as transformative mediation that recreates relationships between individuals and groups in the twenty-first century.

Readers using a womanist hermeneutics of religious ethical mediation ask these questions:

1. How are the characters in the text enmeshed in the omnipresence of violence in their context? What are sources of conflict that sustain the violence in their context?
2. Who are the characters encountering one another, and what conflict ensues from the encounter? Who acts as a religious ethical mediator in the encounter? What does the religious ethical mediator do to redirect energies of conflict from destructive to constructive? Does the character as mediator become a transformative reconciler?
3. How is the context transformed as the characters live into the space between a culture of deception that sustains the omnipresence of violence and a culture of moral courage that is sustained by the omnipresence of God's justice? What ethical meaning and response emerges as the context becomes a site of transformative reconciliation?
4. What can we in the church today learn about living faithfully in the omnipresence of violence within and outside of the church? How do faithful disciples become transformative reconcilers in church and society?

Furthermore, the omnipresence of the justice of God is the counterforce to the omnipresence of violence and context for moral agency. Consequently, the ethical responses to violence should be consistent with "the contours of biblical justice."[38] Biblical justice begins with God because "justice is not something God aspires to; it is the heart of who God is and what God does."[39] There are several ways that we can recognize biblical justice as reasons for ethical

38. Chris Marshall, *The Little Book of Biblical Justice* (Intercourse, PA: Good Books, 2005), 22.
39. Ibid.

actions : (1) to believe in God's justice is to believe in God's faithfulness and have hope; (2) God's justice is a call to action against present injustices; (3) action against injustice is more than maintaining law and order; (4) justice is complex and may sometimes be impartial or partial, and partiality is on the side of the powerless and vulnerable; (5) justice is about relationships between humans and with God; and (6) the fullness of God's justice is restoration.[40]

Because human beings are created in the image of God, we are to be "agents of justice."[41] As agents of justice, our actions may have a variety of consequences that may align with the contours of biblical justice: reparative or punitive (corrects present or past wrongs), compensatory (ensures that everyone receives her or his due), restorative (seeks repair of relationship), and/or distributive (transforms patterns of injustice and creates ongoing equity). In sum, Ruth and Esther are two women who are moral agents of justice challenging gendered violence.

### Specific Questions for Interpreting Ruth and Esther as Religious Ethical Mediators

— How is gendered violence happening in the text?
— What are tensions of encounter (conflicts) that sustain such violence?
— What are ways that Ruth and Esther live as religious ethical mediators transforming violence and reconciling relationships?

These questions are answered in sections entitled religious ethical mediation interpretation by exposing historical or contemporary persons or events that mirror characters, issues, and themes in the texts. I seek to mediate meaning between the text and context, helping the reader of the commentary to grapple for their own meaning for preaching and teaching.

40. Ibid., 27–48.
41. Ibid., 26.

# RUTH

# Introduction to Ruth

> Some texts resist dating at all. Was the book of Ruth written
> during the period of the Judges, which is when the story is set?
> Or was it written while David was attempting to solidify his
> kingship, in order to explain how this Israelite ruler happened
> to have a Moabite great-grandmother? Or was it written com-
> paratively late, during the time following the Babylonian exile,
> when some factions of the community, represented by Ezra
> and Nehemiah, encouraged the divorcing of foreign wives and
> others wanted to show that foreign wives were not only appro-
> priate, but also divinely sanctioned?[1]

This quote points out the various ways by which scholars might
date and understand the purpose of the book of Ruth. Scholars have
dated the book either from King David's era (c. ninth century BCE)
or the early postexilic period (fifth–sixth centuries BCE).[2] Per the
opening lines of the book, the setting of the story is during the time
of the Judges, and this points to the canonical placement of the book
between Judges and Samuel. This placement suggests to the reader
that this story can be a reminder of the connection between law and
faithfulness, "an exilic (or postexilic) hope for the restoration of the
Davidic monarchy," and the function of Judges in Israel's history.[3]

---

1. Douglas A. Knight and Amy-Jill Levine, *The Meaning of the Bible: What the Jewish Scriptures and the Christian Old Testament Can Teach Us* (New York: HarperCollins, 2011), loc. 369 of 9381, Kindle.
2. Judy Fentress-Williams, *Ruth*, Abingdon Old Testament Commentaries (Nashville: Abingdon, 2012), 20–22, Kindle.
3. Arie C. Leder, "Paradise Lost: Reading the former Prophets by the Rivers of Babylon," *Calvin Theological Journal* 37 (2002): 20–22; Carlos Bovell, "Symmetry, Ruth and Canon," *Journal for the Study of the Old Testament* 28, no. 2 (2003):175–91; Charles P. Baylis, "Naomi in the Book

This commentary joins Old Testament feminist biblical scholar Katharine Doob Sakenfeld, who acknowledges the difficulty in dating the book and opts to focus (as other commentators, including rabbis) on "instruction concerning the community's view of outsiders" and how this points to the exclusivism of communities as a perennial challenge to life among diverse groups of people.[4] Along with this focus on the purpose of Ruth, this commentary joins Judy Fentress-Williams, who interprets Ruth through the lens of identity: "the set of characteristics and values that allows a person to be known and identified within a group. These characteristics and values assigned by any given community come out of that community and serve its interests."[5] In this commentary the identities of Ruth, Naomi, and Boaz are critical to the way that the tensions of encounter (relationships and conflicts) between these individuals and the social groups they represent are negotiated and transformed. Likewise, in our time social group identities have become central to debates about identity politics and the public policies that derive from such. As suggested in the introduction to this commentary, Ruth is a book that can help us think through the twenty-first-century versions of problems about how to live together amid pluralism and diversity in US society and around the globe.

Furthermore, there is debate about whether the book was authored by a female. Here again the debate cannot be fully settled; some suggest that a guild of women storytellers may have been responsible for its oral transmission, if not its written version. Also, there are points in the text that are suggestive of a female author: for example, "But Naomi said to her two daughters-in-law, 'Go back each of you to your mother's house'"[6] (1:8a), and the translation of the Hebrew in 1:20b when Naomi names God as El Shaddai, the translation could have been "the breasted one"[7] rather than the Almighty

---

of Ruth in Light of the Mosaic Covenant," *Bibliotheca Sacra* 161 (October–December 2004): 18, 19–22.

4. Katharine Doob Sakenfeld, *Ruth* (Louisville, KY: John Knox, 1999), 4–5.

5. Fentress-Williams, *Ruth*, 24.

6. Amy-Jill Levine, "Ruth," in *Women's Bible Commentary* (Louisville, KY: Westminster John Knox, 1998), 86. Levine notes that the term is found in other passages, such as Gen. 24:28; Song 3:4, 8:2, but various ancient Hebrew translations choose the male-defined expression, *father's house.*

7. Fentress-Williams, *Ruth*, 59.

as in the NRSV. Likewise, the book brings the interests of women to the fore and is characterized by a female worldview. This worldview begins with (1) three women left without their husbands who (2) have different plans for their lives going forward that become the journey of an older woman and a younger woman whereby (3) Ruth offers female companionship while (4) Naomi has to learn to accept the validity of their unconventional partnership, and (5) although marriage to Boaz is central to the women's quality of life, it is a means to an end that (6) eventuates in Israel's female genealogy.

Also, there is a comedic structure to the book. Comedic structure refers to the way that the book of Ruth exhibits the goal of the literary genre of comedy—the transformation of both characters and audience.[8] Using a comedic structure, the book of Ruth introduces an alternate reality: a Moabite woman who demonstrates faithfulness (*hesed*) that transforms the existing reality and relationships. Ruth's faithfulness allows her to escape the role of foreigner/outsider to which she is assigned by cultural norms.[9] More specifically, Fentress-Williams reads the book of Ruth as a "dialogic comedy" because transformation happens through dialogue "between characters in the story and the dialogue between the reader and the text."[10] This dialogical reading is consistent with reading through a womanist hermeneutics of religious ethical mediation.

The debates about dating and authorship provide background that illuminates the book's purpose. Still, it is the understanding of how gendered violence is evidenced in the text that opens up pathways to ethical reflection upon historical and contemporary issues that sustain that violence in our time that are the foci of this commentary. Likewise, the women's worldview and the teachings of the book of Ruth about the tension between inclusivism and exclusivism within community are significant to this commentary's interpretation of the book. The book of Ruth speaks to us theologically and ethically about how (1) women survive and thrive in the face of patriarchal customs and traditions that embed gendered violence and (2) we might live faithfully with different "Others" in the omnipresence of God's justice.

8. Ibid., 17.
9. Ibid.
10. Ibid.

# *Reading Ruth through the Hermeneutics of Religious Ethical Mediation: An Overview*

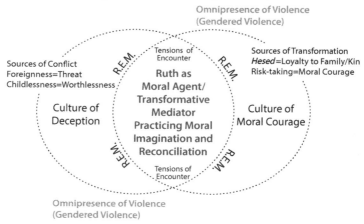

Reading the Book of Ruth through the hermeneutic of religious ethical mediation reveals a context in which gendered violence is assessed through an understanding of the omnipresence of God's justice as God's *hesed* (steadfastness, faithfulness). Despite Naomi's feelings of divine rejection in the face of the loss of her husband and sons, Ruth is a moral agent who mediates the tensions deriving from her foreignness (threat) and Naomi's feelings of worthlessness (childlessness) by making morally courageous decisions. First, Ruth risks rejection by Naomi and her people and accompanies Naomi as she returns to her people. Second, Ruth expresses loyalty to Naomi, even though Naomi does not acknowledge her loyalty. Third, Ruth imagines a familial relationship with Naomi, her God, and her people. Hers is a moral imagination that recognizes the reality of rejection, and still she takes a leap of faith to live into a future where she and Naomi find security. She acts as a transformative mediator/reconciler who enables Boaz to honor marital customs in a new way and ensures that a familial line continues.

# INTRODUCTION TO RUTH

Here you are encouraged to read the story of Ruth as the story of a religious ethical mediator. She lives into the tensions of encounter (dismissal and rejection) as a moral agent who is a risk-taker. Her religious ethical mediation happens from marginalization as the space from which she assesses how to engage the people and context and where faith is lived out; she believes in God's faithfulness to provide resources for survival.

# Ruth 1

## 1:1–5

### *A Family Displaced by Famine*

According to these opening verses, Elimelech has taken his wife and two sons to live in Moab because there is a famine in their homeland, Bethlehem in Judah. Although Elimelech dies, his wife, Naomi, and her sons, Mahlon and Chilion, remain in Moab. In fact, Mahlon and Chilion marry Moabite women named Orpah and Ruth. After ten years, Mahlon and Chilion die. Thus, without the protection of men, Naomi and her two daughters-in-law must each decide about their lives in their patriarchal society (the primary context for gendered violence in this story).

These opening verses provide a context for understanding the immigration of this family to a land associated for Israelites with hostility (Num. 22–24; Judg. 3:12–30) as well as sexual perversity (Gen. 19:30–38) toward the people of the land, the Moabites. In this story, it is significant that two previously estranged groups of people, the Israelites and the Moabites (Num. 25:1–5; Deut. 23:3–6) become intimately connected. Indeed, the two groups become in the end more than simply cohabitants in Moab; they have become family through intermarriage. The story of Elimelech's family and the Moabites that begins here offers a perspective for us during the current massive global migration of peoples. Elimelech knowingly crosses into "enemy" territory so that his family can survive, even though they are *strangers without legal status or rights*. They can be either rejected by the host country because they are strangers or they may be extended hospitality as guests. Moreover, as immigrants because of famine in their homeland, the date or any assurance of their return home is uncertain.

*A Family Displaced by Famine*

> The social matrixes in the book of Ruth are rich. They include male/female, husband/wife, mother/son, mother-in-law/daughter-in-law, owner/oversee/ laborers, mother's house/father's house, native resident/foreigner, and so forth. These relations are forged through marriage, friendship, widowhood, sexual attraction, economic and labor arrangements, immigration and political amity or enmity.
>
> Gale A. Yee, "'She Stood in Tears amid the Alien Corn': Ruth, the Perpetual Foreigner and Model Minority," in *Off the Menu: Asian and Asian North American Women's Religion and Theology*, ed. Rita Nakashima Brock et al. (Louisville, KY: Westminster John Knox, 2007), 52–53.

These introductory verses lead us to ask these questions: Why do people immigrate into hostile territory? What kinds of relationships can be forged between a host country's inhabitants and immigrants?

## FURTHER REFLECTIONS
### *Famine*

Famine is a recurring theme in the Old Testament; it is a reason that patriarchs such as Abraham travel to foreign lands (Gen. 12:10). Drought (Deut. 28:23–24) and a plague of insects that destroy crops (Deut. 28:38–42) lead to famine, and this is reported to be a consequence of Israel's disobedience. Famine thus creates separation from ancestral land, and this separation is tragic because identity is tied to the land. With respect to the events that open the book of Ruth, there is separation from the land and loss of identity for Elimelech's family, who immigrated to Moab because of famine in their land: "The family is the stronghold against death and the family is rooted in the land. In this sense, the removal from the land is more than a precursor of tragedy, it is a tragedy. Seen in this light, the ensuing deaths of the men can be understood as a direct result of being separated from the land."[1]

Also, famine (or scarcity) serves a literary function in biblical texts such as 2 Samuel 21, Ruth 1, and the apocryphal book of Judith. "Each of these stories moves from a state of disequilibrium, marked by death and violence, toward a new equilibrium in which famine

1. Judy Fentress-Williams, *Ruth*, Abingdon Old Testament Commentaries (Nashville: Abingdon, 2012), 42, Kindle.

and conflict are resolved. In each text, women (Naomi, Ruth, Rizpah, and Judith) play key roles in the resolution of these conflicts."[2] In Ruth 1, famine, the reason that the Israelite family immigrates to Moab along with the deaths of Elimelech, Mahlon, and Chilion, sets in motion the story and the conflict to be resolved. Famine and these deaths will find resolution through what happens to Naomi and Ruth on the way to Israel at the time of barley harvest when the law of gleaning comes into play (Lev. 19:9–10 and Deut. 24:19, the law requiring some grain be left unharvested for the poor, aliens, and widows to glean). Biblical traditions and social conflicts with others are evoked by the literary use of the barley harvest: intermarriage (Ezra 9–10), treatment of widows and aliens (Deut. 24), gleaning (Lev. 19 and 23, Deut. 24), levirate marriage (Deut. 25:5–10), covenant language ("steadfast love"), and idealized womanhood (the "woman of substance" of Prov. 31:10 and Ruth 3:11).[3] "Ruth and Naomi's attempt to gain their social position from a recalcitrant Boaz and the next of kin represents a social conflict that must be overcome."[4] The storyline in Ruth moves through famine, death, and the agency of women to mediate this social conflict of gendered violence.

> **The author of the book of Ruth includes elements within the pastoral story that remind readers of the vulnerability and violence just under the surface of Ruth and Naomi's situation.**
>
> Amy C. Cottrill, *Uncovering Violence: Reading Biblical Narratives as an Ethical Project* (Louisville, KY: Westminster John Knox Press, 2021), 98.

## *Religious Ethical Mediation Interpretation*

In the twenty-first century, hunger in the United States and global famine are a lived reality for a large percentage of the world's population.[5] Hunger and food insecurity in the United States continue

---

2. Brian Britt, "Death, Social Conflict, and the Barley Harvest in the Hebrew Bible," *The Journal of Hebrew Scriptures* 5, no. 14 (2005): 3.

3. Ibid., 13–14.

4. Ibid., 16.

5. World Food Program USA, "Global Hunger: 10 Coutries Suffering the Most from Hunger," https://www.worldvision.org/hunger-news-stories/world-hunger-facts; UN World Food Program USA, https://www.wfpusa.org/articles/global-food-crisis-10-countries-suffering -the-most-from-hunger/.

A Family Displaced by Famine

to increase (approximately forty-seven million people) and affect particular social groups (children, seniors, rural communities, African Americans, Latinos) disproportionately.[6] The famine that drove Elimelech and his family to Moab is the result of natural conditions, but sometimes politics and war are the reasons. The important point for ethical reflection is that outcomes preceding from famine in this text remind us that the reasons for the migration (moving within the borders of a home country or across borders) and immigration (moving across borders most often with the intention of settling permanently) of people tend to be beyond their control.

Violent religious and political insurgencies along with economic recessions and natural disasters have fueled massive migrations across the globe. In the politically charged and xenophobic twenty-first century context, there is extremist violence domestically and internationally with which immigrants must contend. It does not seem to matter whether people have immigrated in search of a better life or whether they are refugees escaping persecution; the disdain for them is overwhelming. According to various sources, the global refugee crisis of the twenty-first century is unprecedented. The rapidly escalating figures reflect a world of intractable conflicts, with wars in the Middle East, Africa, Asia, and Europe, driving families and individuals from their homes in desperate flight for safety. But the systems for managing those flows are breaking down. An average of nearly forty-four thousand people a day join the ranks of those either on the move or stranded far from home. The charity Concern Worldwide US reports that

> Over the last few years, we've reported on an unprecedented crisis of both international and internal displacement. Unfortunately, as the UNHCR (United Nations High Commissioner of Refugees) reveals, 2023 did not show any signs of that crisis going away: Over 117 million people were newly displaced last year, as a result of persecution, conflict, violence, and human rights violations (among other causes).
>
> In just a decade, the number of refugees around the world has nearly doubled, and at one point in 2023 we exceeded 40 million refugees around the world. As of the beginning

6. Feeding America, "Hunger in America," https://www.feedingamerica.org/hunger-in-america.

of 2024, the number of refugees under UNHCR protection (accounting for people who returned home over the year) was 37.6 million. The UNHCR estimates that this number will continue to grow this year.[7]

Chinese artist and activist Ai Weiwei's 2017 documentary, *Human Flow*, allows us to see and hear from the people who are suffering displacement from their homelands and the loss of family and friends. In an interview, Weiwei notes that there are seventy nations building fences to close their borders, as compared to eleven during the Cold War era. Furthermore, he reminds us that as attitudes toward refugees and immigrants harden, we should ask ourselves, "Who are we?" By asking this question he says that we are encouraged to judge ourselves and acknowledge that we must all bear responsibility for the human loss of the global refugee crisis.[8] From an ethical point of view, we Christians should ask about how we are complicit in this forced migration and how our frequent failure to be actively in solidarity with immigrants and migrants contributes to twenty-first-century inhumanity to one another.

A couple of examples of migration within and immigration to the United States are informative. In 2005 Hurricane Katrina hit the Gulf Coast; US citizens in New Orleans whose homes were wiped out of existence were forced to seek shelter beyond the borders of the state of Louisiana.[9] Many of the displaced people were African Americans, and they were labeled by the media as refugees. There was much controversy over the use of this term because these individuals and families were indeed US citizens who were displaced by the catastrophic events surrounding Hurricane Katrina, but they were not persons who had crossed an international border or were fleeing persecution.[10] However, some people thought that the

---

7. Concern Worldwide US, "The Global Refugee Crisis, Explained," June 20, 2024, https://concern.net/news/global-refugee-crisis-explained/.

8. CBS News, "Ai Weiwei on 'Human Flow,' Criticizes Hardening Attitudes on Refugees/'We All Bear Responsibility,'" https://www.youtube.com/watch?v=8ltCwIxbUOE.

9. Sarah Pruitt, "Hurricane Katrina: 10 Facts about the Deadly Storm and Its Legacy," History, updated August 27, 2024, https://www.history.com/news/hurricane-katrina-facts-legacy; Danielle Baussan, "When You Can't Go Home," Center for American Progress, August 18, 2015, https://www.americanprogress.org/article/when-you-cant-go-home/#:~:text.

10. United Nations, "About Internally Displaced People: Special Rapporteur on the Human Rights of Internally Displaced Persons," http://www.ohchr.org/EN/Issues/IDPersons/Pages/Issues.aspx.

conditions that created the aftermath of homelessness derived in part from long-term systemic economic injustice and political corruption, and this qualified the Katrina victims to be called refugees.[11]

Likewise, discussion of and debate about immigration to the United States (e.g., from Mexico) exposes the way in which a group of immigrants can be despised and used to supply labor domestically all at the same time. Immigrants are also often scapegoated for the loss of jobs in the United States, although US and multinational corporations choose to transplant their operations to developing countries and exploit the people in those countries by paying lower wages than would be required by law in the United States and in some cases using child labor—something that is illegal here.

The immigration and migration of numerous families in the twenty-first century are forced, like Elimelech and his family, because of natural, political, and/or economic circumstances beyond their control. They are forced by circumstances to choose life in countries that are inhospitable (at best) and hostile (at worst). We Christian readers of the text and global citizens of the twenty-first century should recognize that immigrants and migrants are forced to migrate so that they can survive; indeed, any fear of being exploited and/ or rejected by the country to which they immigrate is overcome by their will to survive.

What do these opening verses say to us Christians about how we might understand and practice hospitality to migrants and immigrants? Most often we think of hospitality as a relationship between a host and guest—a giver and a receiver—and that relationship can turn into paternalism whereby the host extends one-sided charity that does not recognize mutuality between host and guest. Frequently, we act like Naomi, who does not think that this foreign woman Ruth has anything to offer her.

However, hospitality can be a relationship of solidarity. A relationship of solidarity between hosts and guests is based on empathy and mutuality. In solidarity with migrants and immigrants, hosts and

---

11. Cheryl A. Kirk-Duggan, ed., *The Sky Is Crying: Race, Class, and Natural Disaster* (Nashville: Abingdon, 2006). See also *Broken Promises: 2 Years after Katrina*, ACLU Publication, August, 2007, https://www.aclu.org/publications/report-broken-promises-two-years-after -katrina.

guests realize that their fates are interconnected. Feminist theologian Letty Russell's understanding of hospitality affirms this posture of solidarity:

> Just hospitality is the practice of God's welcome by reaching out across difference to participate in God's actions bringing justice and healing in our world of crisis and fear of the ones we call "other." To live out God's welcome as just hospitality is a calling and a challenge. As strangers ourselves, and strangers to so many other people, we have the possibility of partnering with others as a sign of God's concern for us all, and for all creation.[12]

Lastly, although the opening lines of the book tell us that the story takes place in the time of Judges and famine can be a punishment in the Old Testament for Israel's disobedience to the covenant, the text does not cite God explicitly as a cause of the famine that drives Elimelech and his family from home. We must curb our tendencies to theologize natural events or political decisions. Far too often such theologizing is used to diminish human responsibility for or ignore underlying human-driven causes of such events or decisions. We do not want to acknowledge that faulty theologizing protects a privileged way of life for some while producing devastating outcomes for others. For example, current debate about whether global warming is a scientific fact, a political ploy, or God's punishment for declining morality in the United States detracts us from discussing seriously the human destruction of the planet in pursuit of consumer-driven choices for our comfort and convenience. We claim that the theological assertion of humanity's dominion over (power over) God's creation has been displaced by the notion of stewardship (care for). Yet stewardship of the earth has not necessarily translated into behaviors that sustain creation. We still fundamentally want the earth to take care of us. It is time that we remember our intrinsic connection to the earth (not just when we say ashes to ashes, dust to dust on Ash Wednesday or at funerals). We must confess our abuse of the earth through overdependence on fossil fuels and overuse of

---

12. Letty M. Russell, *Just Hospitality* (Louisville, KY: Westminster John Knox Press, 2009), 101, Kindle.

*Three Women in Dialogue about Their Fate*

plastics. Are we prepared to be in a nonviolent relationship with the earth? African environmentalist Wangari Maathai admonishes us:

> Climate change is forcing all of us—rich and poor—to acknowledge that we have reached a point in the evolution of this planet where our needs and wants are outstripping the ability of the earth to provide, and that some of us will have to do with less if those who have very little are going to have enough to survive. It may require a conscious act of some of us saying no in addition to finding other, less destructive ways to say yes.
>
> None of the healing [of the planet] that is necessary is automatic; it will require much work, for the wounds that have been created in the earth are deep. If we can't or won't assist in the earth's healing process, the planet might not take care of us either.[13]

## 1:6–18

### *Three Women in Dialogue about Their Fate*

Naomi hears that the famine is over; "for she had heard in the country of Moab that the Lord had considered his people and given them food" (v. 6b). However, as she and her daughters-in-law are traveling back to the land of Judah, Naomi insists that Orpah and Ruth return to their "mother's house." (v. 8) Orpah decides to return to her family, but Ruth remains and makes a vow to Naomi. The most often quoted part of this vow reads as follows: "Where you go, I will go; where I lodge, you will lodge; your people will be my people, your God, my God" (v. 16).

Naomi gives pragmatic reasons for telling Orpah and Ruth to return to their mother's house: she is widowed, without sons for them to marry, and too old to produce

> **"Both Naomi and Ruth traveled to and lived in foreign countries due to relationships of marriage rather than choice."**
>
> Musa W. Dube, "Diving Ruth for International Relations" in *Other Ways of Reading: African Women and the Bible* (Atlanta: Society of Biblical Literature, 2001), 187.

---

13. Wangari Maathai, *Replenishing the Earth: Spiritual Values for Healing Ourselves and the World* (New York: Doubleday, 2010), 22–23, Kindle.

future husbands (vv. 11–14). Orpah eventually makes her choice to leave Naomi; Ruth decides to stay. Does Ruth decide to stay because she acquiesces to Naomi's interpretation of their dire circumstances? Does she choose to stay because she thinks that life with Naomi will be better than what she's known? What values undergird Ruth's choice?

This dialogue among the women exposes roots of gendered violence. Naomi, Orpah, and Ruth are all widows, but Orpah and Ruth have the additional burden of being women who married foreigners. From Naomi's point of view, the women are trapped by patriarchal norms that tie women's survival to relationships with men. Orpah's decision to return to her people seems a prudent choice from this point of view. Perhaps Orpah decided that her identity was tied to her people and land;[14] the text does not explicitly give us her reason.

Although there is provision for the care of widows and foreign wives under Israelite law, this does not seem to be an immediate reason for Ruth's choice not to return. Is she even aware of this provision? Naomi certainly does not mention it. Instead, in poetic form, it seems that Ruth declares loyalty (a) to Naomi out of love and respect for the mother of her deceased husband and (b) to Naomi's God.

## FURTHER REFLECTIONS
### Ruth's Vow

The story of Ruth has been dramatized for religious and secular audiences.[15] Ruth's vow is probably one of the most familiar passages of Scripture in the Old Testament. The words have been set to music and used in wedding ceremonies.[16]

---

14. Musa W. Dube, "The Unpublished Letters of Orpah to Ruth" in *Ruth and Esther: A Feminist Companion to the Bible*, ed. Athalya Brenner (Sheffield: Sheffield Academic,1999), 145–50. In this article, there is a series of letters that are addressed thus: "To Ruth, Our Youngest Moabite Sister. From Orpah Your Eldest Moabite Sister. I am Orpah, the one who returned to her mother's house and to her Gods." In these letters Orpah says: "But I had to return to my old widowed mother who, like Naomi, did not have any son or husband left. It was also right that I should return to my people and my religion, for Naomi herself was returning to her people and her religion. I have continued in this court as the regent queen and priestess."
15. "Story of Ruth-Movie HD," YouTube, https://www.youtube.com/watch?v=PPjEY3F8gHs; http://www.imdb.com/title/tt0400330/?ref_=ttfc_fc_tt.
16. "Wherever You Go," sung by the monks of the Weston Priory, https://www.youtube.com/watch?v=yGn3uENUEec.

*Three Women in Dialogue about Their Fate*

Some feminist interpretation focuses on Ruth's vow through the lens of women's love for women and as an example of women's solidarity. Feminist Rebecca Alpert discusses Ruth and Naomi's love for one another as women through Jewish lesbian women's experience. Alpert says that "this story of female friendship resonates powerfully with Jewish lesbians in search of role models. Ruth and Naomi have a committed relationship that crosses the boundaries of age, nationality, and religion."[17] She asserts that a Jewish lesbian midrash on Ruth makes it plausible to imagine that Ruth and Naomi become lovers. The plausibility of this midrash follows from these points (1) there is no prohibition in the Hebrew Bible against lesbian sex; (2) although Jewish legal texts do prohibit lesbian sexual practice between married women, Ruth's marriage to Boaz is to protect their relationship; and (3) the story is from an oral tradition of women storytellers. Most importantly, Alpert asserts, "It is not the goal of midrash to prove the story actually happened this way, but to make room for change within tradition while providing historical antecedent for change. Making room for lesbian interpretations of the Book of Ruth is a way of welcoming lesbians into the contemporary Jewish community."[18] Still, the issue is how to include the stranger who is among the community yet experiencing exclusion. Heteropatriarchal norms for relationships override any imperative to be community.

17. Rebecca Alpert, "Finding Our Past: A Lesbian Interpretation of the Book of Ruth," in *Reading Ruth: Contemporary Women Reclaim a Sacred Story*, ed. Judith A. Kates and Gail Twersky Reimer (New York: Ballantine Books, 1996), 93.
18. Alpert, "Finding Our Past," 96–97. Cf. Madipoane Masenya (ngwan'a Mphahlele), "Engaging with the Book of Ruth as Single, African Christian Women: One African Woman's Reflection," *Verbum et Ecclesia* 34, no. 1 (September 30, 2013), https://verbumetecclesia.org.za/index.php/VE/article/view/771. In this article, Masenya reflects on the meaning of Ruth in a Bible study with women who belong to one of the traditional South African Pentecostal churches, asking whether the story of Ruth is affirming or disaffirming. The author suggests that Alpert's reading of Ruth may be helpful in affirming "affectionate female relationships" within some African contexts, such as *metsoalle* and mummy-baby dyads of Lesotho and the Zande women of Sudan. She asserts, "An important question to be posed mainly to the ecclesial community, and particularly to those who are invested with the power to interpret the Word, who seldom offer concrete alternative solutions regarding the sexual needs of single women: could the *metsoalle* relationships, and their affirmation by Alpert's (1996: 91–96) reading of the Naomi-Ruth story, serve as model for many single women to imitate without condemnation?," 8. Revised as "Rebecca Alpert's Lesbian Reading of the Book of Ruth within the *Metsoalle* Context of Lesotho," *Journal of Gender and Religion in Africa* 18:1 (July 2012): 43–62.

Aruna Gnanadason invites readers to consider Ruth and Naomi's relationship as a story of solidarity that different social groups of women might emulate. In a Bible study, she emphasizes the "change of heart and consciousness" that Naomi must undergo on the way to such solidarity. Gnanadason explores "from a post-colonial perspective, the potential of this story, to help us forge bonds of unity among women within nations and across continents, overcoming many historical obstacles in our way."[19] Reading Ruth through the lens of two Indian narratives, she exposes the gendered violence of women missionaries as they pushed evangelical ideals that denigrated Indian religion and women. As the missionaries worked to overthrow "paganism," they converted masses of Dalit women and reinforced caste and class divisions among women simultaneously.[20] Missionaries even challenged an Indian law of inheritance that allowed the succession of property through female lines rather than male lines; this "heathenish" law was replaced by the Christian law of inheritance whereby fathers bequeath land to sons. In the face of this history and the continuing experience of oppression of Dalit women through "public forms of social violence" and the abuse from upper-caste men and women, Gnanadason asserts the usefulness of the story of Ruth and Naomi thus: "We need a new political and theological imagination to reclaim the power of our sisterhood—the sisterhood between Naomi and Ruth—to get more actively engaged in transformation of all injustice in our societies and the world."[21]

However, confessing to unjust imperialistic missionary practices must precede any efforts to be in solidarity. Efforts to be in solidarity will be part of a long process toward forgiveness that includes confession and apology, perhaps even reparational justice. If we take seriously the history of oppressive missionary activity and want to atone for the damage that was done in the name of spreading the gospel, we might reimagine the Great Commission as a practice of

---

19. Aruna Gnanadason, "Ruth and Naomi—Making Their Story of Solidarity Our Story," in *Righting Her-Story: Caribbean Women Encounter the Bible Story*, ed. Patricia Sheerattan-Bisnauth (Geneva: World Communion of Reformed Churches, 2011), 77.
20. Ibid., 255. "Dalits– refer to those communities that were considered untouchable in the Indian caste system."
21. Ibid., 89.

religious ethical mediation. This means that we begin from a committed but not absolutist religious posture. We are committed to the gospel, but are we willing to be self-critical about why we want to spread the good news? If we are living in the omnipresence of God's justice, then, even as missionaries, we are to do so as agents of God's justice rather than agents of a denomination.

Womanist biblical scholar Yolanda Norton writes about the assimilationist tendency of the book of Ruth: "the text masquerades as a treatise on the inclusion of the other, instead the book seems to be more of a commentary on the assumed virtue of membership and participation in the Israelite community."[22] Norton also points out a tension in the narrative between "the hegemonic impulse to promote social accommodation and subservience on the part of the oppressed" and "the ways in which the marginalized take agency and save themselves."[23] So, the question remains: Does Ruth's vow to Naomi mean that the value that Ruth chooses is assimilation? When Ruth makes her vow to Naomi, she does seem to express more than a desire to be solely in a relationship of friendship or lesbianism with Naomi. Ruth is also making a religious commitment. However, Norton notes that Ruth's bold declaration of allegiance silences Naomi. Norton offers two possible reasons for Naomi's silence to Ruth's expression of loyalty: (1) Ruth the Moabite will be a "social liability" upon her return and or (2) "she felt entitled to Ruth's deference and thus it held no value for her."[24] Norton's interpretation presents us readers with another dilemma for Ruth that complicates her agency as a religious ethical mediator. Will she succumb to assimilation?

### Religious Ethical Mediation Interpretation

Ruth's vow must be interpreted against the backdrop of Israelite-Moabite intermarriage. If this intermarriage is understood as an idyllic relationship forged between two foreigners, then the reader might

---

22. Yolanda Norton, "Silenced Struggles for Survival: Finding Life and Death in the Book of Ruth," in *I Found God in Me: A Womanist Biblical Hermeneutics Reader*, ed. Mitzi J. Smith (Eugene, OR: Cascade, 2015), 265.

23. Ibid., 266.

24. Ibid, 268–69.

be inclined toward either Alpert's or Gnanadason's interpretation of the relationship between Ruth and Naomi. If Ruth 1:4 is translated "They-abducted for-themselves Moabite women,"[25] then the intermarriage is another example of gendered violence in this context. It is important thus to consider the weight of the choices (what motivates each woman's choice) made by Orpah and Ruth. Orpah may or may not be fully accepted upon her return home; some might embrace this injured daughter with compassion because of her abduction, and others might shun her as a defiled woman because of her marriage to a foreigner. Ruth may have weighed the possibility of rejection upon returning to her family and Moab and decided to take her chances with Naomi. Ruth cannot be certain that Naomi is on her side given that Naomi does not offer a reciprocal declaration of loyalty or gratitude for Ruth's vow. Also, Ruth must be painfully aware that she will have to prove herself: in spite of the declaration of complete allegiance to Naomi, her people, and her God.

Now, let's interpret the vow through Ruth's uncertainty and painful awareness. Ruth chooses to interpret the bond in a way that contradicts traditional norms for a foreigner and a woman's place in society. Ruth's choice signals her agency. Ruth chooses to be a moral agent who will act as a transformative mediator/reconciler in this context of gendered violence. Loyalty is the virtue of character driving Ruth's choice. And, because she makes this choice painfully aware of its implications, Ruth is living into the space of moral courage, and she will need moral imagination in order not to become a pawn of her circumstances. This is a space of uncertainty where she will mediate between the cultures of deception and moral courage, which in her context of gendered violence must be navigated through tensions arising from foreignness, male childlessness, and loyalty to one's people and religion.

---

25. Wil Gafney, "Ruth," in *The Africana Bible: Reading Israel's Scriptures from Africa and the African Diaspora*, ed. Hugh R. Page Jr. et al. (Minneapolis: Fortress, 2010), 250–52. Gafney says "there are at least three indicators that Ruth was abducted into marriage: (1) the use of the verb *ns'*, 'lift,' with 'woman,' instead of the standard *lcqh*, 'take (as wife), (2) the long-standing Israelite practice of abduction or rape-marriage, and (3) the preferential abduction of foreign women for rape-marriages. The verb in Ruth 1:4, *vayis'u*, from *ns'*, 'to lift' or 'pickup,' may be taken to indicate that Ruth and Orpah, both Moabite women, were abducted into marriage."

*Three Women in Dialogue about Their Fate*                                    **39**

# FURTHER REFLECTIONS
## *Hesed*

Ruth's vow is about *hesed*:

> The Hebrew term for the kind of extraordinary behavior witnessed in this story is *hesed*, usually translated "kindness" or "loyalty" in the NRSV. The Hebrew term is a strong one. It refers to care or concern for another with whom one is in relationship, but care that specifically takes shape in action to rescue the other from a situation of desperate need, and when the rescuer is uniquely qualified to do what is needed.[26]

In this interpretation of Ruth's vow, *hesed*, enacted by Ruth, cannot be separated from her moral agency of risk-taking, an act of loyalty, consistent with living as a religious ethical mediator who acts as a transformer of conflict and reconciler of relationship amid tensions of intercultural encounter. In one sense, Ruth is uniquely qualified to rescue Naomi: Ruth is younger and therefore may provide a male heir as a route back into social standing for Naomi and, perhaps, standing for herself, within the Israelite community. In another sense, it is not so much that Ruth is uniquely qualified to be Naomi's rescuer as it is that she is *willing* to do so. When Ruth proclaims loyalty to Naomi, her people, and her God (vv. 16–18), she asserts her moral agency as *hesed (loyalty), which in this setting is a form of risk-taking deriving from moral imagination: that is, Ruth is willing to imagine life beyond the current circumstances that threaten their survival and limit the women's life choices.* Ruth is a moral agent because she is motivated by an assessment of the women's circumstances and envisions a purpose for their lives as women that is not limited to or, at least, will not be fulfilled solely by what culture or tradition dictates.

## *Religious Ethical Mediation*

Racial-ethnic persons of color constantly make Ruth's choice. We live in a society and world where educational credentials, social prestige, and/or political power are never enough to be fully accepted

26. Katharine Doob Sakenfeld, *Ruth* (Louisville, KY: John Knox, 1999), 11–12.

in historically white educational or religious institutions, the professional athletic world, and/or even the presidency of the United States. Our choices have been circumscribed by laws, customs, and color-based stereotypes, and racial-ethnic women of color have been additionally denigrated by negative sexualized myths about our bodies and character. Still, we choose to risk being ignored and silenced (at best) and beaten and killed (at worst), claim our humanity, and practice moral courage as risk-taking rather than acquiescing to discriminatory uncertainties in the present because we fear perpetual unjust future outcomes.

## 1:19–22

### *Naomi and Ruth Arrive in Bethlehem*

The arrival of Naomi and Ruth generates a commotion, and the women of the city ask, "Is this Naomi?" Perhaps the question stems from the fact that Naomi is accompanied by an unknown person rather than returning with the family with whom she had departed. Or perhaps Naomi is unrecognizable because she carries herself as one aged and burdened by loss or fear about how she will be received. Naomi responds to the women's question by complaining about the way that God has dealt harshly with her; she asks to be known from this point forward as Mara (meaning bitter) because of her bitterness about her barrenness. There is no query about Ruth.

### *Religious Ethical Mediation Interpretation*

Naomi's tirade against God as she renames herself makes explicit her experience of God as that of absence and abandonment. Again Naomi is silent with respect to Ruth. Their arrival at the beginning of barley harvest is not acknowledged by Naomi as a sign that God has not, in fact, deserted her. Naomi and the women of the city ignore Ruth and become complicit in the gendered violence of othering some women into invisibility. Women's captivity to gendered violence, or differently worded, women's internationalization of gender oppression is an ethical challenge when we think of socialization as

*Naomi and Ruth Arrive in Bethlehem*

a lifetime process.[27] Some ethical questions are these: How do we counter-socialize all of us from complicity with gender oppression into values that nurture gender justice? What are the spaces and contexts of counter-socialization where we teach and learn values that are central to accepting, protecting, and loving the stranger (vulnerable immigrants, marginalized women) as one's neighbor? How do we ensure that these spaces and contexts do not become *places of equally oppressive progressive extremism* where only certain interpretations of acceptance and liberation are considered legitimate?

## FURTHER REFLECTIONS
### *Identity*

Feminist Judy Fentress-Williams uses "identity as a primary lens for interpretation," and her insights provide an overarching framework for reflection in this section.[28] She says "identity is a construct formed by culture that serves a purpose. Identity determines who is an insider and who is an outsider."[29] Ruth's presence with Naomi cannot be acknowledged because it blurs the insider-outsider clarity that makes the community whole. Also, to acknowledge Ruth is to have historical amnesia about the relationship between Israel and Moab. "Historically, the Moabites are not harmless outsiders; they are a threat to core practices of Israel, that is, worship of YHWH alone. They are associated with forbidden worship practices. God severely punished the people for intermarriage with Moabite women that resulted in the worship of false gods (Num. 25)."[30] Because of Ruth's vow we know that she has chosen to accept Naomi's God.

Consequently, both Naomi and Ruth are grappling with their identities. Naomi is seeking to reclaim an identity as she returns to her people and homeland. Ruth is constructing a new identity as a Moabite among people who have demonized her people of origin.

27. Arthur Brittan and Mary Maynard, *Sexism, Racism and Oppression* (New York: Basil Blackwell, 1984), 85–86.
28. Fentress-Williams, *Ruth*, 24.
29. Ibid.
30. Ibid, 28.

## Naomi

In a study of Naomi from the perspective of the Mosaic covenant, Naomi is cognizant of markers of her identity relative to being one of Israel's people. In her opening dialogue with Orpah and Ruth, her reasons for them not to return with her allude to levirate marriage law in Deuteronomy 25. She has no more sons (brothers of Mahlon and Chilion) for them to marry legally in Israel. Likewise, Naomi is compelled into silence after Ruth makes her vow because she recognizes that vow as consistent with a Mosaic covenant provision regarding the power of vows to bring blessing or curse (Deut. 23:21–23).[31] Naomi's struggle with her identity is twofold. First, she struggles to define herself and reintegrate into the Israelite community. This interpersonal relationship with Ruth that Ruth has sealed with a vow complicates matters. Second, upon arrival in Bethlehem, Naomi chooses a new name, Mara, that reflects her condition—her bitterness about returning home as a barren widow. (v. 21) This outburst makes explicit the way Naomi is concerned about how the biological and social expectations that provide women social standing in the community are barriers to inclusion. Thinking about Fentress-Williams's definition of identity, Naomi is an insider who defines herself through the norms of covenantal relationship and by her disappointment with the way that the covenant has not protected her—"Call me no longer Naomi (pleasant), call me Mara (bitter), for the Almighty has dealt bitterly with me" (v. 20). She is an insider who feels like an outsider.

Feminist Jacqueline Lapsley asks us to consider the book of Ruth as the story of Naomi's predicament as much as it is Ruth's story. Lapsley pushes for a cultural and ideological critique that reminds interpreters not to dismiss assertive and older women. She encourages us to see and hear Naomi. Readers are to look beyond the title of the book and not be caught in the snare of the failure of most interpreters who overlook Naomi.[32] Lapsley invites us to consider

---

31. Charles P. Baylis, "Naomi in the Book of Ruth in Light of the Mosaic Covenant," *Bibliotheca Sacra* 161 (October–December 2004): 422–25.

32. Jacqueline Lapsley, "Seeing the Older Woman: Naomi in High Definition," in *Engaging the Bible in a Gendered World*, ed. Linda Day and Carolyn Pressler (Louisville, KY: Westminster John Knox Press, 2006), 106.

# Naomi and Ruth Arrive in Bethlehem

Naomi's identity as a function of the way that she relates to God; like Job she complains vehemently to God—that God caused her to leave home and left her bereft of family.[33] Thus, if we see and hear Naomi, then we see her as an outspoken older woman who is remaking her identity and life just as Ruth is con-

> **Naomi assimilates into the world of Israelite men, the landowners who possess the means of production, while the foreign female worker, Ruth, vanishes when her body is exhausted.**
>
> Gale A. Yee, "'She Stood in Tears,'" 60.

structing one. Differently from Ruth, though, Naomi does so within parameters of privilege.

## Ruth

Ruth's quest for identity begins with her vow to Naomi, formally extending her familial relationship as daughter-in-law to becoming a member of the covenant community as she declares loyalty to Naomi's people and God.[34] As Ruth encounters Boaz, another level of membership in the covenant community is initiated. Ruth—the foreigner—is declared by Boaz "a woman of valor" (Ruth 3:11; Prov. 12:4; 31:10); when he marries her and she gives birth to a son, her identity takes on the character of being a full-fledged member of the community.[35] Some maintain that this act of allegiance and identity formation is itself an act of violence, especially when identity is contingent upon acceptance of monotheism.[36] Ruth's allegiance to Naomi amounts to conversion to the Israelite faith, and that requires her to forget both her gods and her family.

Postcolonial feminist Eunny P. Lee describes the tension between kinship and otherness that earmarks both (a) Naomi and Ruth's relationship and (b) Ruth's identity—she is the Moabite, the daughter-in-law, the widow of Mahlon. Lee speaks of Ruth's "hybridity" and "the attendant tension between foreignness and

---

33. Ibid., 107–13.
34. Cf. Arie C. Leder, "Paradise Lost: Reading the Former Prophets by the Rivers of Babylon," *Calvin Theological Journal* 37 (2002): 17–22.
35. Ronald T. Hyman, "Questions and Changing Identity in the Book of Ruth," *Union Seminary Quarterly Review* 38 (1984):194–200.
36. Regina M. Schwartz, *The Curse of Cain: The Violent Legacy of Monotheism* (Chicago: University of Chicago Press, 1997), as cited in Kwok Pui-lan, *Postcolonial Imagination and Feminist Theology* (Louisville, KY: Westminster John Knox Press, 2005), 114–16.

familiarity."[37] Indeed, there are three times when Ruth's identity is questioned explicitly: "To whom does this young woman belong?" (2:5), "Who are you?" (3:9), and "How did things go with you, my daughter?" (3:16). These questions and the answers to them hold kinship-otherness tension intact. In the first instance, the servants answer in terms of Ruth's ethnicity—"the Moabite who came back with Naomi from the country of Moab" (2:6); second, Ruth claims a self-identity—"I am Ruth, your servant" (3:9a); and the third question contains Naomi's affirmation of the identity of Ruth as her daughter-in-law. The answers to these questions reveal and reinforce Ruth's imposed identity as widow and daughter-in-law deriving from her relationship to Naomi and her emergent self-understanding in those roles.[38] Importantly, though, from the moment that Ruth decides to stay with Naomi her identity is subversive.

> **Ruth is a subversive character in that she subverts gender and ethnic boundaries through her actions.**
>
> Sarojini Nadar in *Other Ways of Reading: African Women and the Bible*, 171

### *Religious Ethical Mediation Interpretation*

When we readers enter this scene with Naomi and Ruth we have already heard Ruth profess her loyalty to Naomi and allegiance to Naomi's people and God. Perhaps some of us are taken aback by the way that Naomi apparently ignores Ruth now that she is in the presence of women like herself. Perhaps others of us live as Ruth, frequently pushed aside by women with whom we have worked in solidarity for sexual-gender justice in church and society. The interpretation of this text must mediate the textual and current reality of women's complicity with gendered violence as oppressors of other women. Complicity with sexual, gender, or racial oppression signifies the tension individuals experience because of a need to be accepted for fear of being rejected by a reference group (family,

---

37. Eunny P. Lee, "Ruth the Moabite: Identity, Kinship, and Otherness," in *Engaging the Bible in a Gendered World*, ed. Linda Day and Carolyn Pressler (Louisville, KY: Westminster John Knox Press, 2006), 92, 93.
38. Ibid, 94–100.

*Naomi and Ruth Arrive in Bethlehem*

friends, sexual-gender group, racial-ethnic group, socioeconomic group). Ruth mediates the acceptance-fear tension; she chooses to stay with Naomi, to forge a relationship rather than be defined by the other women of Bethlehem and the religio-social norms that exclude her as a foreigner.

Still, this question seems to plague Ruth's identity: Is Ruth's ethnicity as a Moabite diminished or annihilated by her full-fledged vow? If this is a story about assimilation (as suggested by Norton above), then, perhaps, the intent is to annihilate her ethnicity through a series of religio-cultural transitions so that the reader will accept her role in the genealogy that concludes the book. If this is a story about radical inclusion of an outsider into the covenant community, then, perhaps, the intent is to shift the focus onto how covenant functions: "Ruth reminds her audiences that YHWH's people are not only chosen, but they must also choose YHWH"[39]—as Ruth has done. Ruth comes to the covenant community with her identity as a Moabite, and this identity remains intact even as she vows allegiance. Her loyalty does not require that she exchange one identity for another but that she live with integrity, faithful to her vow, in this new community. Ruth's ability to stand by her vow of loyalty to Naomi and her God while being ignored and rendered silent as an outsider offers a lesson about integrity from which we can learn. Integrity is measured by the ability to honor the commitments that you make. Integrity is needed to act in spite of the ways that others may assess one's choices and actions. Living as a religious ethical mediator requires the kind of integrity that Ruth lives out.

39. Fentress-Williams, *Ruth,* 57.

# Ruth 2

## 2:1–3

### *Gleaning in the Fields*

The narrator opens chapter 2 by informing us that Naomi has a rich kinsman of the family of Elimelech named Boaz. Now, consistent with Ruth's pledge to Naomi, Ruth volunteers to go into the field to glean to provide for them, and she is beginning to envision a larger plan: "Let me go to the field and glean among the ears of grain, behind someone in whose sight I may find favor" (v. 2a).

## 2:4–17

### *Boaz's Introduction to Ruth*

When Boaz sees this unfamiliar woman, he inquires of the servant in charge of the reapers, "To whom does this young woman belong?" (v. 5). The servant informs him that this is the Moabite who returned with Naomi and tells how Ruth has worked without a break from early in the morning. Boaz then speaks directly to Ruth; he gives her permission to glean only in his field and tells her that he has ordered the young men not to bother her (v. 9).

A dialogue between Ruth and Boaz follows in which she inquires about why he has taken notice of her: "Why have I found favor in your sight, that you should take notice of me, when I am a foreigner?" (v. 10; and see v. 13). Boaz discloses that he knows how she has cared for Naomi as well as the fact that she left her family and homeland: "May the LORD reward you for your deeds, and may you have a full reward from the LORD, the God of Israel, under whose wings you have come for refuge!" (v. 12).

*Encouraged to Continue Gleaning*

## 2:18–23

### *Encouraged to Continue Gleaning*

Later Boaz invites Ruth to eat with his household and then gives instruction to the young men to allow her to glean even among the standing sheaves (v. 16). In the conversation with Naomi upon her return from the fields, Ruth is informed that Boaz is a "relative of ours, one of our nearest kin" (v. 20). Ruth recounts for Naomi the day's events, and Naomi encourages her to continue gleaning in Boaz's fields. Ruth gleans until the end of the barley and wheat harvests, living with and providing for her mother-in-law.

### *Religious Ethical Mediation Interpretation*

Several tensions of gendered violence are presented in these verses. First, the notion of women as property (e.g. Boaz's inquiry about to whom Ruth belongs) is exposed. Second, a contemporary reader should ask questions about the fine line between a woman's use of seduction as a survival strategy—a need to survive her circumstances or as a personal choice about how she shall choose to use her body and sexuality to engage in the world. In the present world of gendered violence, it is difficult to imagine authentic freedom of choice for women regarding their bodies. Third, readers should grapple with how the actions of the women implicate them in gendered violence (i.e., Naomi's encouragement for Ruth to engage Boaz). These exposed tensions are not new to life within a patriarchal society. What seems new, or at least different, is the way that Boaz responds to Ruth. He is inquisitive about Ruth followed by being protective toward Ruth, and finally he is generous and hospitable. Although the narrator tells us who Boaz is, the story proceeds as if neither Boaz nor Ruth know the specific role that Boaz can play in these women's lives; Ruth is informed by Naomi that he is a relative after Ruth's encounter with Boaz (v. 20). Therefore, what is the reason for Boaz's generosity and hospitality toward Ruth? Or, should his actions even be characterized as generosity and hospitality?

# FURTHER REFLECTIONS
## *Gleaning*

*The Gleaners* by Jean-Francois Millet is an oil painting of three women gleaning in a field that depicts what has been described as three phases of womanhood—young, middle aged, elderly. Some think that the young woman in the painting is Ruth, and she is described as beautiful, exhibiting poise as she gleans in comparison to the labored efforts of the other two women.[1] Perhaps Ruth's youthful appearance and agility in gleaning is a first reason that Ruth catches Boaz's eye, or it might be because she seems out of place because of her ethnicity. Of course, the text tells us that his servant informs Boaz that this woman is the Moabite who returned with Naomi. Boaz then remarks to Ruth that it is because of all that she has done for Naomi as well as her acceptance of their religion that he admires her (v. 11).

Millet's painting depicts the fields as serene and pastoral, but more recent translations of the text (2:9, 22) assert the harvest fields "as a potential source of physical and even sexual endangerment for Ruth."[2] These revised translations speak of warnings from Naomi and Boaz to Ruth in terms of the possibility of being molested in the fields. "Thus, a more explicitly aggressive rendering of the verbs (e.g. by 'molest,' 'assault') attests to a new tradition of English translating that is more attuned than ever before to the social phenomenon of violence against women."[3]

More specifically, when Ruth is permitted to glean, one of two Israelite laws that applied to foreignness and poverty appear to come into play. As has already been noted, Israel's relationship to Moab is filled with animosity and disdain (Gen. 19:30–38; Num. 22–24; 25:1–5; Deut. 23:5). So in chapter 2, it is Ruth's foreignness that is accentuated as she gains legal status under the protection of Israelite law as an alien. (Lev. 19:9–10; Deut. 23:22; 24:19–22).[4]

1. "The Gleaners by Jean-Frncois Millet," YouTube, https://www.youtube.com/watch?v=5g3mt7AiAtw.
2. David Shepherd, "Violence in the Fields? Translating, Reading, and Revising in Ruth 2," *Catholic Biblical Quarterly* 63 (2001): 458.
3. Ibid., 459–60.
4. Agnethe Siquans, "Foreignness and Poverty in the Book of Ruth: A Legal Way for a Poor

> **The insidious economic picture that surfaces in the book of Ruth is that the Israelites—in the persons of Naomi and Boaz—are those who do not work, who exploit and live off the surplus labor of the foreign Other.**
>
> Gale A. Yee, "'She Stood in Tears amid the Alien Corn': Ruth, the Perpetual Foreigner and Model Minority," in *Off the Menu: Asian and Asian North American Women's Religion and Theology*, ed. Rita Nakashima Brock et al. (Louisville, KY: Westminster John Knox Press, 2007), 60.

Gleaning is clearly a means of economic survival for these two vulnerable women, but it is a "short-term solution"[5] that will be addressed more in the next chapter when the second Israelite law, levirate marriage, offers the final solution.

## Religious Ethical Mediation Interpretation

Feminist Old Testament scholar Katharine Sakenfeld offers a couple of contemporary examples that she thinks parallel the experience of gleaning. First, there are welfare programs that aid poor and unemployed people in the United States; women and children are disproportionately among those who need and receive these benefits. Second, in some rural areas in developing countries, poor people glean after corporate farms complete their mechanical harvesting.[6]

Moreover, in their context Naomi and Ruth are both a vulnerable and protected class; they are a widow and a foreigner who seek and find assistance and asylum among the Israelites because of some of their laws. In today's social context of gendered violence, women are still vulnerable for similar reasons (race or ethnicity, singleness, poverty), but our laws are becoming less able to protect us. Women's vulnerability and likelihood of protection are also tied to social statuses and identities ascribed to them, such as being put on a pedestal (labeled a trophy wife), or membership in the pecking order of social groups of women driven by race-ethnicity and socioeconomic class. For example, arbitrarily imposed standards for beauty (such as white or light skin, skinny hips, pointed nose, blue eyes, straight hair) persist as well as attacks on the character of individual women and groups of women of color who are judged relative to

---

Foreign Woman to Be Integrated into Israel," *Journal of Biblical Literature* 128, no. 3 (2009): 443–48.

5. Katharine Doob Sakenfeld, *Just Wives? Stories of Power and Survival in the Old Testament and Today* (Louisville, KY: Westminster John Knox Press, 2003), 32.

6. Ibid., 32–33.

those standards. These standards of beauty persist even as women of color and women of different physical body types are in the public eye as recognized leaders in medicine, business, politics, sports, music, and other endeavors. It is the public comments about these women on social media and other platforms that reveals a continued racist normativity of whiteness as the marker of beauty. This comment on Facebook about First Lady Michelle Obama is a prime example of the above assertions: "It will be refreshing to have a classy, beautiful, dignified first lady in the White House. I'm tired of seeing a Ape in heels."[7] Likewise, Serena Williams, a four-time Olympic gold medalist and holder of more Grand Slam titles than any other tennis player, has been labeled savage and manly. In fact, a reporter asked if she was intimidated by her white opponent, Maria Sharapova's "supermodel good looks."[8]

Are women truly a protected class against gender discrimination and violence today? Public policy debates over sexual harassment and assault of women in society and on college campuses continues to rage regardless of legal protections such as rape shield laws and Title IX of the Education Amendments. Likewise debates before and after the repeal of *Roe v. Wade* in June 2022 hold in tension these kinds of assumptions: (a) protecting women's right to choose is a matter of ensuring control over their bodies; (b) protecting women is about restraining them from misguided decision-making; and (c) protecting women is about keeping women from putting personal choice above the divine mandate to procreate the human species. The tensions between vulnerability, exploitation, and protection in women's lives are part and parcel of both the biblical and contemporary contexts.

---

7. BBC News, "Michelle Obama 'Ape in Heels' Post Causes Outrage," November 17, 2016, https://www.bbc.com/news/election-us-2016-37985967.
8. Talia Smith, "Serena Williams, Body Shaming, and the White Gaze," *Paper*, June 4, 2018, https://www.papermag.com/serena-williams-body-shaming#rebelltitem2.

# Ruth 3

## 3:1–5

### *Naomi and Ruth in Partnership*

Now, fully embracing her role as mother-in-law, Naomi instructs Ruth on how to approach Boaz, and the plan is set in motion: a permanent solution to their survival and economic woes. Interestingly, Naomi speaks of seeking "security" so that it "may be well" (v. 1) with Ruth. At the heart of this planned encounter with Boaz is the instruction to lie with him as he sleeps (v. 4).

## 3:6–15

### *Ruth's Nighttime Encounter with Boaz*

Ruth now has a nighttime encounter with Boaz following the guidance of Naomi. The intended result of the plan is for Boaz to marry Ruth. Although Ruth's preparation for meeting Boaz is characterized by washing and anointing herself as would a bride, the nighttime encounter is intimate and may have been sexual given the use of feet in biblical texts as a euphemism for the penis (vv. 6–9). In fact, Boaz remarks: "May you be blessed by the LORD, my daughter; this last instance of your loyalty is better than the first; you have not gone after young men, whether poor or rich. And now, my daughter, do not be afraid, I will do for you all that you ask, for all the assembly of my people know that you are a worthy woman" (vv. 10–11).

There is a glitch; Boaz discloses that there is another kinsman who is entitled to carry out the duties of the next of kin. Still, though, Boaz asserts that he will act as her next of kin if the closer relative refuses. Boaz sends Ruth back to Naomi with six measures of barley for Naomi before he departs for the city (vv. 12–15).

## 3:16–18
### *An Unsettled Matter*

After Ruth tells Naomi what transpired between she and Boaz, the chapter ends with Naomi advising Ruth to await the final disposition of the matter as to who will serve as the next of kin.

### *Religious Ethical Mediation Interpretation*

What accounts for the shift in Naomi's attitude toward Ruth? (3:1: "Naomi her mother-in-law said to her, '*My daughter, I need to seek some security for you, so that it may be well with you*'" [emphasis added].) Naomi's language about Ruth bespeaks of Naomi's embrace of Ruth as family. Is Naomi's attitudinal shift a matter of self-interest, or has she truly come to *accept* Ruth and sees their fates as interdependent? Or is it best to simply remember that Naomi needs to survive, and Ruth is her only certain ally by default (from Naomi's point of view) or choice (from Ruth's point of view)?

What about Boaz? His attitude toward Ruth seems to derive from the way he sees her fulfilling the role of daughter-in-law and as an "adopted" member of the community. Boaz is also somewhat flattered by Ruth's choice of him, and this motivates him to fulfill communal, covenantal expectations as much as anything else. What can we learn from Boaz about mixed motivations and making ethical choices?

The relationship between Naomi and Ruth is complicated by their age differences, the circumstances that brought them together, expectations imposed upon them because of their gender, and covenantal obligations to fulfill as members of the Israelite community. In the first and second chapters, Naomi ignores and then accepts Ruth reluctantly, although all along she has been accepting the beneficence of Ruth. Here in chapter 3 she accepts Ruth in the role of daughter-in-law.

*An Unsettled Matter*

Anna May Say Pa sheds interesting light on the mother-in-law/daughter-in-law relationship. Naomi and Ruth's relationship is scrutinized through the experiences of Burmese Christian women. Using the cultural experiences of this social group of women, the author questions whether the story of Ruth offers a model of womanhood that liberates or reinscribes an oppressive model of submissive womanhood. Within church settings, Ruth is held up as a model of loyalty, commitment, and obedience, and Burmese Christian women are expected to do likewise in serving their mothers-in-law. "Wenh-In Ng says, 'To have Whither thou goest, I will go held up as one's model from the pulpit when one's culture already demands that you do, is far from liberating.'"[1] Although there are specific cultural experiences and expectations for Asian women that are biblically justified using the Naomi-Ruth relationship, these same values are still taught in many conservative Christian circles in various parts of the world, and the behavior of all women continues to be scrutinized by the covert ideological norms of domestic womanhood, deriving from the nineteenth century cult of domesticity. Whether we in the US churches teach implicitly or explicitly values of submission and obedience using Naomi and Ruth as exemplars, we should be reminded to ask ourselves, Which texts do we choose to teach girls and women Christian standards of behavior? How many sermons are preached or how much pastoral advice is given that supports the subjugation of women in situations of domestic violence, either insisting on the sanctity of the marriage or the need to forgive an abuser?

Feminist, womanist, postcolonial readings of the relationship between Naomi and Ruth offer other interesting ways to interpret what happens in chapter 3. Sarojini Nadar sees Ruth as one who subverts Naomi's instructions and uses the religious language of her adopted religion to push Boaz to honor religious commitments. Naomi seems to instruct Ruth to seduce (sexually or not) Boaz at night on the threshing floor, but while Ruth carries out the instruction, she makes explicit to Boaz the meaning of this seduction: "He said, who are you?" And she answered, "I am Ruth, your servant;

---

1. Anna May Say Pa, "Reading Ruth 3:1–5 from an Asian Woman's Perspective," in *Engaging the Bible in a Gendered World*, ed. Linda Day and Carolyn Pressler (Louisville, KY: Westminster John Knox Press, 2006), 58.

spread your cloak over your servant, for you are next-of-kin." (v. 9) Nadar sums up the matter thus: "Without having to sacrifice her own dignity in the process, Ruth drives the situation to ensure her own survival and simultaneously to gain her rightful place in the Israelite community. Ruth is ensuring that she can progress from outsider to insider."[2] According to Nadar, an equally intriguing part of Ruth's boldness is that she is reinterpreting Israelite law regarding levirate marriage. Ruth is still a foreigner, and the law does not mention marriage to foreigners. Further discussion of levirate marriage follows below.

Ruth 3 can be read as a "counter-type scene" to betrothal-type scenes according to Johanna W. H. Bos. Earmarks of a counter-type scene are (1) a foreign element, (2) an encounter between a male and female initiated by a woman, (3) the encounter involves deception of some sort, (4) the encounter results in some sort of gift, and (5) the woman leaves the place of encounter, and success is announced. Bos highlights how Ruth makes an "autonomous choice" (not dependent on someone else's authority) and how that choice advances God's agenda rather than the patriarchy.[3] Naomi and Ruth's relationship is described as an alliance that joins "weakness to weakness, death to death" because of the vulnerability of their circumstance as a widow and a foreigner. When Ruth encounters Boaz under the cover of night on the threshing floor she affirms her personhood—"I am Ruth, your servant" and takes the initiative to claim a relationship with him—"for you are next of kin." Boaz responds affirmatively to Ruth and gives her a gift to take to Naomi. (vv. 10–15a) Ruth returns to Naomi and announces success. All five elements of the counter-type scene are thus fulfilled.

Some readers may be uneasy with the apparent manipulation that surrounds the women's plan and Ruth's approach to Boaz. Womanist biblical scholar Yolanda Norton sheds light on Ruth's action as consistent with the "trickster"—a biblical motif in the Hebrew Bible

---

2. Sarojini Nadar, "A South African Indian Womanist Reading of the Character of Ruth," in *Other Ways of Reading: African Women and the Bible*, ed. Musa W. Dube (Atlanta: Society of Biblical Literature, 2001), 161–64, 169.

3. Johanna W. H. Bos, "Out of the Shadows: Genesis 38; Judges 4:17–22; Ruth 3," *Semeia* 42 (1988): 38–40.

*An Unsettled Matter*                                                         **55**

and Black culture.[4] A trickster thinks of and uses options outside of conventional or traditional practices to survive in hostile and/or marginalizing circumstances. Norton compares Ruth's experience and actions to those of African American women who frequently must find "subversive modes of navigating foreign spheres for the sake of their own survival."[5] Ruth, like many African American women, acts from a posture of "subversive acquiescence" that is consistent with a worldview of "traditional communalism," holding communal interests above those of the individual. "From the perspective of this narrative, it suggests that ingrained in this Moabite woman's consciousness is a concern for her familial community. She does not have the luxury of caring only for herself."[6] She and Naomi are now family, or at least fictive kin,[7] and Ruth will do what is needful for her family to survive.

Likewise, the trickster's deception offers a lens for understanding the work of transformative mediation. "Trickster myths are useful because they show ways of transiting boundaries and balancing needs that wind circuitously through conflicts, matching the dodges and defenses of parties with windows and possibilities."[8] Transformative mediators know that conflicts are complex, and the mediator, like the trickster, is a boundary crosser (between self and others), shape-shifter (plays many roles), creative disrupter (sees unproductive patterns and makes new choices), peacemaker (looks for redemptive spaces), and storyteller (makes new stories with givens).[9] Alongside these features of the trickster, conflict transformation acknowledges the uses of constructive deception (aiding in self-determination and informed decisions), as opposed to

---

4. Yolanda Norton, "Silenced Struggles for Survival: Finding Life in Death in the Book of Ruth," in *I Found God in Me: A Womanist Biblical Hermeneutics Reader*, ed. Mitzi J. Smith (Eugene, OR: Cascade, 2015), 269.

5. Ibid., 270.

6. Ibid., 270–71.

7. Prince Kumar, "Fictive Kinship: Social Bonds beyond Blood and Marriage," Sociology Institute, November 1, 2022, https://sociology.institute/sociology-of-kinship/fictive-kinship-social-bonds-beyond-blood-marriage/

8. Michelle LeBaron, "Trickster, Mediator's Friend," in *Bringing Peace into the Room: How the Personal Qualities of the Mediator Impact the Process of Conflict Resolution*, ed. Daniel Bowling and David Hoffman (San Francisco: Jossey Bass, 2003), 137.

9. Ibid, 140–47.

destructive deception (done for the gain of one at the expense of others).[10] As explained earlier, in the religious ethical mediation framework, the context for moral agency consists of a culture of deception and a culture of moral courage. When choices or actions arise in the culture of deception, the deceptive outcomes are destructive. Constructive deception arises in the culture of moral courage and is used in the pursuit of a reevaluation, reconsideration, or transformation of choices or actions. A mediator may use constructive deception, like a trickster, to create collaborative process.[11] Ruth, the religious ethical mediator here, collaborates with Naomi in a plan that they hope will open Boaz up to new options in relation to Ruth.

Two postcolonial readings reflect upon the relationship between Naomi and Ruth through the experiences of trafficking of women and girls in Malawi and the situation of foreign, female migrant workers in contemporary Israel.[12] In the first instance, Ruth is cast as a young woman trafficked by Naomi; "Naomi uses Ruth's beauty and youth as potential for reclaiming her property and decent livelihood."[13] In the second case, the experiences of migrant workers in Israel and Ruth's experience are read bidirectionally. This means that each experience sheds light on the other; migrant workers and Ruth have no choice, foreignness is ever the earmark of identity. The female migrant worker like Ruth works in the fields, marries a rich local, and has his child; this alters the worker's civil, civic, and social status. Still, Ruth, the migrant worker, is not integrated, only assimilated, and even religious conversion does not mean full acceptance.[14]

In sum, Ruth and Naomi's relationship upon the return to Judah exposes several attitudinal shifts and tensions of encounter that require mediation. Naomi's attitudes toward Ruth seem in flux as Naomi grapples to comprehend the meaning of her life post-famine

10. Robert D. Benjamin, "Managing the Natural Energy of Conflict: Mediators, Tricksters, and the Constructive Uses of Deception," in *Bringing Peace into the Room: How the Personal Qualities of the Mediator Impact the Process of Conflict Resolution*, ed. Daniel Bowling and David Hoffman (San Francisco: Jossey Bass, 2003), 124.

11. Ibid., 125–30.

12. Respectively, Fulata Lusungu Moyo, "'Traffic Violations': Hospitality, Foreignness, and Exploitation: A Contextual Biblical Study of Ruth," *Journal of Feminist Studies in Religion* 32:2 (2016): 83–94; and Athalya Brenner, "From Ruth to the 'Global Woman': Social and Legal Aspects," *Interpretation* 64:2 (April 2016): 162–67.

13. Moyo, "'Traffic Violations,'" 91.

14. Brenner, "From Ruth to the 'Global Woman,'" 167–68.

*An Unsettled Matter*                                                    **57**

as well as who she is upon arriving back home to her people. She seems to tolerate Ruth at first because of the vow, then embraces or uses her in the role of daughter-in-law. As daughter-in-law, Ruth is embraced or used finally as the one who can rescue them; they collaborate, or Ruth concedes to a plan concerning Boaz. Ruth's attitude toward Naomi appears consistently one of dedication to her mother-in-law—from her vow to gleaning in the fields to following Naomi's instructions about how to approach Boaz. As Ruth gets closer to fulfilling fully her duty to Naomi, it is not so much her attitude as an expectation of full acceptance by Naomi that comes into play.

Boaz's attitude toward Ruth is at first one of curiosity, then he admires her loyalty to Naomi, and finally he has desire for her on the threshing floor. His admiration and desire lead to a willingness to fulfill a covenant obligation. From this last perspective, Boaz's hospitality and generosity are genuine, though his motivations are mixed. Like any of us, he makes an ethical choice, fulfilling the demands of covenant (obligation) as he understands such, but his motivations for that choice are a mixture of egoism and altruism. He needs the attention and affection of the younger woman, and he wants genuinely to help Naomi and Ruth out of his wealth and abundance.

Ruth is at the heart of all the shifts in attitude as an initiator of relationships (her vow to Naomi, her calling upon Boaz to fulfill his role as next of kin). She mediates difference and transforms the relationships of otherness into ones of recognition. Consequently, she, Naomi, and Boaz are empowered to act on behalf of self and one another. Perhaps what transpires between Ruth, Naomi, and Boaz offers us an illustration of loving one another interdependently.

Because of the individuals involved, these shifts in attitude signify tensions of intercultural encounter among the three players—Naomi, Ruth, and Boaz—in this drama. First, there is an interreligious, interethnic tension. Second, there is an intergenerational tension. Third, there is a tension of gender expectations that characterizes both the relationship between women and the relationship between women and men. Finally, there is tension between tradition and countertradition. Again, Ruth is the mediator of these tensions; she takes risks rooted in her allegiance to both Naomi and faith in Naomi's God. She exercises insight and good judgment in the fields, on the threshing floor, and with respect to gendered oppression, all for the sake of reconciling an estranged woman, Naomi—to herself and her people.

# Ruth 4

## 4:1–2
### *Waiting for the Next-of-Kin*

Boaz arrives at the city gate as Elimelech's next of kin is passing by. In the company of the elders, Boaz tells the first next of kin that Naomi is selling a parcel of land that he can redeem or Boaz will.

## 4:3–6
### *Who Will Be the Redeemer?*

After the first next of kin agrees to redeem it, Boaz informs him that he will also acquire Ruth the Moabite and maintain the dead man's line of inheritance. The first next of kin now withdraws his offer of redemption and grants his "right of redemption" to Boaz.

## 4:7–10
### *Boaz Is Declared the Redeemer*

This transaction is confirmed with the custom of removing his sandal and giving it to Boaz before the elders and all the people: "Today you are witnesses that I have acquired from the hand of Naomi all that belonged to Elimelech and all that belonged to Chilion and Mahlon. I have also acquired Ruth the Moabite, the wife of Mahlon, to be my wife, to maintain the dead man's name on his inheritance, in order that the name of the dead may not be cut off from his kindred and from the gate of his native place; today you are witnesses" (vv. 9–10).

# 4:11–12

### *A Prayer and Blessing for the Marriage of Boaz and Ruth*

The people and elders, as witnesses, acknowledge the inheritance and marriage as they pray: "May the LORD make the woman who is coming into your house like Rachel and Leah, who together built up the house of Israel. May you produce children in Ephrathah and bestow a name in Bethlehem; and through the children that the LORD will give you by this young woman, may your house be like the house of Perez, whom Tamar bore to Judah" (vv. 11–12). The blessing brings matters full circle as it foretells the future. The family line that was broken by famine and death can now continue. The blessing compares Ruth to Rachel, Leah, and Tamar; the link to Tamar is of interest in the following way:

> Tamar, like Ruth, goes to some lengths to preserve the line. Both stories involve levirate marriage, both raise the question of identity, and both involve a sexual encounter that is planned by a woman. Perhaps, the blessing is identifying Ruth as someone who has broken through the barriers of cultural norms, like Perez (Tamar's son), who broke through to claim the birthright. Here that act is blessed by the elders of community and Ruth, the woman coming into the house of Boaz, is blessed as well.[1]

The building up of Israel—the continuation of a line of descendants—is what is at stake (2 Sam. 7:27), and "the phrasing of the people's blessing in Ruth foreshadows the eventual rise of David's line and points to the references to him in the concluding verses of the story."[2] Witnesses are needed to complete the legal transaction and its attendant moral obligation as well as to pray for the future outcome of such.

### *Religious Ethical Mediation Interpretation*

This chapter opens with Boaz fulfilling his promise to Ruth to serve as next of kin. The acquisition of some land belonging to Elimelech makes possible the marriage to Ruth. This transaction is to be

---

1. Judy Fentress-Williams, *Ruth*, Abingdon Old Testament Commentaries (Nashville: Abingdon, 2012), 118–19, Kindle.
2. Katharine Doob Sakenfeld, *Ruth* (Louisville, KY: John Knox, 1999), 77.

A Prayer and Blessing for the Marriage of Boaz and Ruth

undertaken by the next of kin, who has the legal right of redemption. Boaz is not the first next of kin. So Boaz waits at the gate until the first kinsmen comes along so he can claim his legal right to acquire the land. The kinsman is willing to do so until Boaz mentions that attaining the land means that he must also marry "Ruth the Moabite" (v. 5). Thinking about how this acquisition will negatively impact his inheritance, the kinsman relinquishes his right of redemption. Although redemption here refers to the acquisition of land to ensure the line of Elimelech, this act of redemption is not unlike Ruth's action on behalf of Naomi. As Ruth fulfills her vow, she rescues Naomi and redeems the line of Elimelech. Ruth rescues Naomi through her vow as an act of *hesed*. Boaz now is rescuing both Naomi and Ruth through the legal right of redemption. Drawing this parallel between the actions of Ruth and Boaz is an interpretative move that pushes some exploratory questions regarding the theological meaning of redemption in the book of Ruth: What roles do humans play in God's redemption of humanity? What does it mean to fulfill such a role? What are characteristic traits of human redeemers?

These verses bring us full circle with Ruth on the journey from Moab to Judah. Ruth now fulfills her vow as she becomes Naomi's surrogate. Does this surrogacy truly end the struggle for survival and full acceptance by Naomi or integration into the community? Are there indicators that Israel is now a community of inclusion?

## FURTHER REFLECTIONS
### *Levirate Marriage and the Redemption of Land*

Levirate marriage is a law of ancient Israel that protects the lineage and land of a tribe. The legal requirements of this law are found in Deuteronomy 25:5–10. According to the passage in Deuteronomy, the husband's brother is to marry his brother's wife upon the death of the brother who has no son (v. 5). The reason for this arrangement is to provide an heir, and the first born of this marriage will carry the name of the deceased (v. 6). If the brother refuses to perform this duty, the elders will summon him, and in their presence the wife will remove his sandal (a symbolic renunciation of the land), spit in his face, and say: "This is what is done to the man who does not build up his brother's house." (v. 9) The brother is thus shamed publicly, and the wife of the deceased is now relegated to the impoverished—the resident aliens, the orphans, and the widows.

Biblical scholars have studied and compared the different ways levirate marriage is a legal transaction in Deuteronomy 25:1–10, Genesis 38, and Ruth 4, including its relationship to incest prohibitions in Leviticus 18 and 20. Some scholars do describe the event at the gate between Boaz and the unnamed next of kin as a legal transaction confirmed by the removal of sandal from the latter to the former. Others question whether the event in Ruth 4 is, in fact, about the legal transaction to confirm levirate marriage or a countertradition. After all, there is no actual provision for foreign wives in the tradition. Although Ruth is designated "the widow of the dead man" (v. 15a). "Strictly speaking, although this legal construction is not in full accordance with the law, it does not contradict it either. However, this new interpretation is *halakah* in favor of the two women without husbands."[3] Both women as widows are afforded legal status whereby Ruth can take Naomi's place in the levirate marriage to Boaz; Ruth is Naomi's surrogate.

Scholars discussing the transaction in 4:3–6 note difficulties within the passage: "The actual conversation between Boaz and the next-of-kin raises vastly more difficult questions about the Israelite customs and the legal and moral rights and obligations presumed in this exchange."[4] Two issues will be highlighted here. First, there is an interesting entanglement of legal right (redeem the land) and moral obligation (marry Ruth to continue the line of Elimelech). Boaz merges these two when he tells

> **The book of Ruth tells readers that the Torah is able to transform even a poor foreign woman without a husband into the great-grandmother of the most famous king of Israel.**
>
> Agnethe Siquans, "Foreignness and Poverty in the Book of Ruth: A Legal Way for a Poor Foreign Woman to be Integrated into Israel," *Journal of Biblical Literature* 128, no. 3 (2009): 452.

---

3. Agnethe Siquans, "Foreignness and Poverty in the Book of Ruth: A Legal Way for a Poor Foreign Woman to Be Integrated into Israel," *Journal of Biblical Literature* 128:3 (2009): 450–51. Cf. Dvora E. Weisberg, "The Widow of Our Discontent: Levirate Marriage in the Bible and Ancient Israel," *Journal for the Study of the Old Testament* 28:4 (2004): 403–29.

4. Sakenfeld, *Ruth*, 70.

*Ruth Bears a Son*                                                        **63**

the kinsman that he must marry Ruth to acquire the land. Second, Boaz uses the same verb, to acquire (Hebrew *qnh*) for the land and for marrying Ruth. In brief, (1) normally the verb for redeem does not apply to marriage, so its use here is unique, and (2) Boaz has not previously spoken about Ruth throughout the narrative in ways that relegate her to the status of property as suggested by applying the verb "acquire" to marriage. Instead, the application of the verb is a rhetorical strategy to place emphasis upon how Boaz has fulfilled his promise to resolve this matter for Ruth.[5]

## 4:13–17

### *Ruth Bears a Son*

Ruth becomes Boaz's wife, is blessed by the Lord to conceive, and she bears a son. The women speak again to Naomi saying, "your daughter-in-law who loves you, who is more to you than seven sons, has borne him" (v. 15b). The son that Ruth has borne is both a gift to Naomi ("a restorer of life and a nourisher of your old age" [v. 15a]) and to Israel. The women declare: "'A son has been born to Naomi.' They named him Obed; he became the father of Jesse, the father of David" (v. 17). There are several interesting points about these verses. First, this is only the second time in the book that God is mentioned as a direct actor (cf. 1:6; 4:13). Naomi's anger at God is reversed fully by God's action with Ruth. Second, the women now extol Ruth, speaking of her loyalty to Naomi as greater than that of seven sons. "The placing of Ruth above the value of seven sons gives the strongest possible cultural expression of her worth in a society that placed such great value upon male offspring."[6] Third, the child is described as "a restorer of life." This idiom has a variety of literal and figurative meanings: (a) physical restoration (Job 33:30), (b) the effect of food in the face of starvation (Lam. 1:11, 19), (c) comforter, restoring courage (Lam.1:16), (d) like God's law that revives the soul (Ps. 19:7), and (e) God as the restorer of soul

5. Ibid., 73–74.
6. Ibid., 82.

**64**　　　　　　　　　　　　　　　　　　　　　RUTH 4:18–22

(Ps. 23:3).[7] Fourth, this short genealogy presents "the mantle of the matriarchs."[8] Reading the blessing intra-biblically, allusions emerge:

1. Ruth and Naomi, like Rachel and Leah, offer examples of females who collaborate.
2. Ruth and Rachel are central to the household.
3. Ruth, like Tamar, is not an Israelite, and both become members of the community against resistance; both provide a critical part of the genealogy that leads to David.[9]

Likewise, one is reminded of God's intervention in Sarah's conception (Gen. 21:1), and Hannah is told by Elkanah that she is better than ten sons (1 Sam. 1:8); then God intervenes and gives her a child.[10] Importantly, the genealogy continues and reveals the identity construction of Ruth as one who marries into the family of Israel because of her loyalty and the risk-taking of *hesed*.

In brief, "Whether Ruth was composed in the period of Judges or later, there is no doubt that the Matriarchs of Israel had already achieved canonical status as models of character. No mode or praise more fitting or biblical could be imagined than associating the Moabite girl with the Matriarchs."[11] Still, Ruth is an outsider whose inclusion is premised upon her usefulness to the needs of the dominant community. As is often the case with gendered violence, the categorial imperative to never treat a person as means to an end is subverted by the need to uphold a patriarchal system through, in this case, this marginalized woman's reproductive capacity.

# 4:18–22

### *The Genealogy of David*

The book concludes with a longer genealogy of David from Perez to David. Boaz is seventh in the list, and David is tenth in the list. In Near Eastern tradition, the seventh and tenth positions signify

---

7. Ibid., 81.
8. Alan T. Levenson, "The Mantle of the Matriarchs: Ruth: 11–15," *Jewish Bible Quarterly* 38:4 (2010): 237.
9. Ibid., 239.
10. Ibid., 240.
11. Ibid., 242.

*The Genealogy of David* 65

special honor, thus the line through Boaz establishes the house of David. Also, this genealogy links the early Pentateuchal stories of Israel to the establishment of the monarchy.[12]

### Religious Ethical Mediation Interpretation

In these concluding verses to the book of Ruth, Ruth is acted upon (Ruth is blessed by God and conceives a son) and overlooked while being praised for what she has done for Naomi (the women again speak directly to Naomi), as well as left out along with any other women in the longer genealogy that lists only fathers and sons. Is Ruth still marginalized by the insiders even as she is central to continuation of the community? Do outsiders ever truly become insiders? Does a community need clear boundaries to exist, or can the borders of community be permeable? What makes community possible?

The journey of Naomi and Ruth comes to an exemplary end. The women are no longer uncertain about their survival. On one hand, this final chapter is a fitting conclusion to a story whose purpose is to make a case for including outsiders in the community of Israel. Sakenfeld offers a wholistic reading of chapter 4. This reading discloses a vision of eschatological hope wherein a community flourishes in these ways:

— Reciprocal movement from margin to center and from center to margin
— Racial/ethnic inclusiveness
— Adequate physical sustenance for all
— Upright individuals together creating and affirming justice and mercy
— Weeping turns to joy, tears are wiped away
— Children are valued and old people are well cared for
— A daughter is greatly valued[13]

---

12. Sakenfeld, *Ruth*, 85.
13. Katharine Doob Sakenfeld, "Ruth 4, An Image of Eschatological Hope," in *Liberating Eschatology: Essays in Honor of Letty M. Russell*, ed. Margaret A. Farley and Serene Jones (Louisville, KY: Westminster John Knox Press, 1999), 63.

From the perspective of religious ethical mediation, this final chapter continues to expose some continuing tensions in the quest to be inclusive community. Ruth and Naomi remain embedded in the gendered violence of a patriarchal context that values them in relation to men as wives and mothers. Likewise, the violence of exclusion because of religious and ethnic difference that Ruth experiences continues as marginalization—the son, Obed, is named by the women of the community (v. 17), and he is handed over to Naomi (v. 16). There is unclarity in the text about what Naomi and Ruth's actual roles in raising the child are, and the following two interpretations must be considered.

First, in "The Story of Ruth, in Three Poems," Erika Dreifus gives us a poignant portrayal of the effects of continuing marginalization upon Ruth and how Ruth serves as "a surrogate for Naomi's redemption" or "a sacrifice for the social mobility of Naomi."[14]

Second, she poignantly gives voice to Ruth's inner thoughts as "Ruth's Regret" in the third poem:"I'd not relinquish my child. Not without regret so strong that it paralyzes and silences me. Forever."[15] Third, "Ruth stands perpetually outside of the communal structure of Israel, only able to achieve superficial recognition for her fertility and devotion. Consequently, at the end of the narrative she is still a Moabite acquisition (4:10) in a public transaction."[16]

> The violence of the book of Ruth is perhaps most directly visible in places that involve Ruth's identity as a Moabite woman. In other words, the potential violence that runs as an undercurrent breaks the surface of the narrative, though not explosively, in situations that involve Ruth's identity as a Moabite and a woman. The gender-related vulnerability that Ruth encounters, though it does not erupt into immediate physical violence, is violent nonetheless.
>
> Amy C. Cottrill, *Uncovering Violence, Reading Biblical Narratives as an Ethical Project* (Louisville, KY: Westminster John Knox Press, 2021), 103, Kindle.

14. Yolanda Norton, "Silenced Struggles for Survival: Finding Life in Death in the Book of Ruth," in *I Found God in Me: A Womanist Biblical Hermeneutics Reader*, ed. Mitzi J. Smith (Eugene, OR: Cascade, 2015), 274, 275.
15. Erika Dreifus, "The Story of Ruth in Three Poems," *Tablet*, June 9, 2016, http://www .tabletmag.com/scroll/204824/the-story-of-ruth-in-three-poems.
16. Norton, "Silenced Struggles," 278.

*The Genealogy of David*                                             **67**

From the perspective of womanist religious ethical mediation interpretation, these last two interpretations remind us that chapter 4 is not meant to resolve the many dimensions of gendered violence that are found throughout the narrative. There are interpersonal, communal, religious-cultural, sexual, and economic tensions that compose the omnipresence of gendered violence in the story. Ruth and Naomi are women social actors and moral agents who must mediate these tensions using strategies of resistance and compliance as well as manipulation and moral courage.

Everything happens in and confirms the omnipresence of God's *hesed* (faithfulness). "God's *hesed*, or faithfulness, by definition, crosses boundaries in its desire to be in relationship with God's creation. Thus, the faithfulness of Ruth crosses the boundaries of land in chapter 1, family in chapter 2, propriety in chapter 3, and history in chapter 4."[17] God's faithfulness is about redemption and justice. Indeed, here redemption is restorative justice enacted through Ruth who is a redeemer/rescuer for the individual Naomi and, at the same time, a transformative reconciler within the community. Her human acts of redemption are both possible and sustained by God whose justice includes making the Creation whole.

Ruth is a foreigner who lives into the tensions of encounter deriving from cultural norms about foreigners as threat. Ruth is a woman who lives into the tensions of cultural norms of childlessness as worthlessness. She has loyalty and risk-taking as primary values at the core of her moral agency as a transformative mediator/reconciler of these tensions. Her moral imagination compels her to fulfill the vow of loyalty to a woman who ignores her and a community who has animosity toward her people of origin. The story of Ruth teaches us that reconciliation is a journey undertaken by faith, by humans whose motivations are mixed, and in the presence of God who calls upon us humans to do our part in the transformation of interpersonal and communal relationships—to do our part in the work of redemption.

---

17. Fentress-Williams, *Ruth*, 131–32.

# ESTHER

# Introduction to Esther

The book of Esther is a challenging text. Readers expect God to be a primary actor in biblical stories, but in Esther there is no explicit reference to God. Also, the final chapters of the book are filled with preemptive or retaliatory violence and that is not the last word that we want to affirm. Still, because the book is in the canon, we must discern its meaning for twenty-first-century Christians who are confronted by issues such as ethnic hate crimes, sexual exploitation, and preemptive or retaliatory violence. The story of Esther might shed light on these issues.

Ruth, Ecclesiastes, and Esther have been described as counter voices from the Megilloth.[1] "Each book brings challenge to normative views: Ruth to the Law, Ecclesiastes to wisdom, and Esther to the absence of God. The three draw readers into their struggles with the nature of God, the expectations of human action, and the role of chance in life."[2] A few evident earmarks of Ruth and Esther as counter voices are these: (1) only two women for whom books of the Hebrew Bible are named; (2) both are stories of survival—survival of a family (Ruth), survival of a people (Esther); (3) both challenge cultural and religious norms for women; (4) they are strangers in their contexts. Likewise, reading the two books as parables highlights their meaning for us today. "The books of Ruth and Esther

---

1. The Megilloth (meaning five scrolls) comprises Ruth, Song of Songs, Ecclesiastes (Qoheleth), Lamentations, and Esther. These five books are traditionally read during holidays in Jewish communities.
2. Kandy Queen-Sutherland, "Ruth, Qoheleth, and Esther: Counter Voices from the Megilloth," *Perspectives in Religious Studies* 3:2 (Summer 2016): 227.

personify the struggles of real-life situations. They challenge tradition and custom and push the boundaries of law and wisdom."[3]

According to Esther 2:7, Hadassah is Esther's Jewish name. Hadassah derives from Hebrew *hadas* ("myrtle or pleasing scent") and is a symbol of love and marriage and perhaps signifies the fate that awaits her. Esther means "star" and is associated with Ishtar, goddess of war and sexual love. "Esther" is also related to the Hebrew *hester* which means "hiddenness," and this certainly points to the way she conceals her identity.[4]

Although the placement of Esther in the Christian canon (after Ezra and Nehemiah—texts that concern the Persian period) as well as details of the period found in the opening verses to the chapter concur with dating the book during the Persian period,[5] there is debate about this. This debate is often linked to discussions of the genre of the book. Douglas Knight and Amy-Jill Levine assert that stories such as Esther and Daniel represent the genre of the court tale that served the following purpose:

> By depicting Jews in intimate, prolonged contact with Gentiles, the writers explored the question of their national identity even as they encouraged readers to maintain it. By presenting the Jews in the context of the court, and thus with access to political power, they offered an optimistic sense that one could thrive apart from Judah and thereby witness to the nations. The court tales of Esther and Daniel combine the humorous and the macabre, the tragic and the joyous. They portray both the real threats to community existence and a remarkably healthy, robust sense of identity.[6]

Likewise, Esther is also described as historical fiction. As historical fiction, Esther draws upon elements from or that are consistent with history, thus lending a sense of historical credibility to the story. Or the book may be described as "a 'novella' of a particular type, a

3. Ibid., 236.

4. Ericka Shawndricka Dunbar, *Trafficking Hadassah: Collective Trauma, Cultural Memory, and Identity in the Book of Esther and in the African Diaspora* (New York: Routledge, 2022), 65, 66–67.

5. For the concurrence of the book of Esther with the Persian period, see Patricia K. Tull, *Esther and Ruth* (Louisville, KY: Westminster John Knox Press, 2003), 12–13, Kindle.

6. Douglas A. Knight and Amy-Jill Levine, *The Meaning of the Bible: What the Jewish Scriptures and the Christian Old Testament Can Teach Us* (New York: HarperOne, 2011), 376, Kindle.

harsh, near-ribald satire on the excesses, brutality, arbitrariness, and shallowness of the rulers of the great Persian empire. This novella incorporates startlingly strong and subversive societal critiques just below the surface of the told tale."[7] Or is it political satire? In the case of Esther, truth is disclosed as the story unfolds around "politics, religious identity, ethics, and gender relations."[8] It is a book that suggests how people in exile both survive and thrive.

## *Reading Esther through the Hermeneutics of Religious Ethical Mediation: An Overview*

Reading the book of Esther through the religious ethical mediation hermeneutic discloses a context filled with gendered, ethnic, and religious violence within an understanding of God's justice as an aspect of God's providence. Here providential refers to God as present (acknowledged or unacknowledged by humans). In other words, the fact that God is not mentioned explicitly in the text does not

---

7. Sylvia Barack Fishman, "Reading Esther: Cultural Impact on Responses to Biblical Heroines" (working paper, Hadassah International Research Institute on Jewish Women at Brandeis University, February 2002), 7.
8. Ibid.

> Christian theologians identify the three elements of divine providence as (1) the preservation of the existence of the universe and all life within it, (2) divine concurrence in human action, and (3) divine concurrence that moves history toward a planned end. The story of Esther illustrates all three of these elements to some extent, but especially draws our attention to the latter two.
>
> Karen H. Jobes, *The NIV Application Commentary: Esther* (Grand Rapids: Zondervan, 1999), 232.

erase God's presence as part of the perspective that can inform our reading of the text. In brief, "in this narrative divine providence—including the reversal of powerful human intentions—is accomplished through the human agency of its endangered heroine."[9] Ruth is a story about the role that humans play in God's work of redemption; Esther is a story about how human actions may or may not align with God's providential justice.

The narrative has four major plot moves: (1) Vashti's banishment, (2) Esther's becoming queen, (3) story of Mordecai saving the king, and (4) Esther's saving of Mordecai and her people.[10] This story is one filled with the dynamics of patriarchal privilege and power, xenophobia, the conflation of law and ethics—all sources of conflict that generate choices and actions consistent with a culture of destructive deception. Likewise, resistance to oppression—choosing to make moral choices amid ambiguity and for the sake of group solidarity—are sources for transformation that foster a culture of moral courage. Esther is becoming a religious ethical mediator who holds in tension the meaning of her womanhood and her Jewish identity as an individual and on behalf of her people through imaginative thinking and empowering actions that disarm King Ahasuerus and Haman, thus she becomes a catalyst for communal liberation of the Jewish people.

> [The book of Esther] addresses gender and power issues as well as the interrelationship of divine intervention by a "hidden God" and human agency.
>
> Dorothy Bea Akoto (nee Abutiate) in *The Africana Bible: Reading Israel's Scriptures from African and the African Diaspora*, ed. Hugh R. Page Jr. (Minneapolis: Fortress, 2010), 268.

9. Fishman, "Reading Esther," 10.

10. Susan Niditch, "Esther: Folklore, Wisdom, Feminism and Authority," in *A Feminist Companion to Esther, Judith and Susanna*, ed. Athalya Brenner (Sheffield: Sheffield Academic, 1995), 32.

# Esther 1

## 1:1–9

### *Extravagance and Excess*

During the third year of his reign, King Ahasuerus, ruler of 127 provinces from India to Ethiopia, sits on his throne in the citadel of Susa and entertains his officials and ministers at a banquet. For 180 days, the king impresses these guests with his wealth and the grandeur of his kingdom. After this banquet, King Ahasuerus holds a second banquet for seven days, and all the men of Susa are invited. Lavish displays of royalty and wealth adorn the court in the garden of the king's palace. Likewise, the royal wine is served and drunk without restraint, "for the king had given orders to all the officials of his palace to do as each one desired" (v. 8b). Meanwhile, verse 9 states that Queen Vashti gave a banquet for the women in the palace. The opening verses of the first chapter set up a theme of excess that runs throughout the book of Esther. Here the excess is about someone in power magnifying his power and wealth through material consumption without limits (in this case, wine is consumed wantonly). All the king's ministers and officials as well as all the men of Susa are invited to royal banquets; is this an act of hospitality or a means to consolidate further monarchial and patriarchal power?

> All of these details signify hegemonic masculinity: the power to rule, control, and dominate; elaborate material possessions; and the ability to drink excessively.
>
> Erika Shawndricka Dunbar, *Trafficking Hadassah: Collective Trauma, Cultural Memory, and Identity in the Book of Esther and in the African Diaspora* (New York: Routledge, 2022), 36, Kindle.

## 1:10–22

### *Male Power—Female Resistance*

As this second banquet is concluding, the king commanded the seven eunuchs who attended him "to bring Queen Vashti before the king, wearing the royal crown, in order to show the peoples and the officials her beauty; for she was fair to behold" (v. 11). Queen Vashti refuses and the king is furious. After consulting others about how to respond legally to the queen, it is decided that Queen Vashti's refusal to honor the king's request is not only an affront to the king but can have widespread social consequences. If her behavior becomes known, then it could encourage all women in the provinces "to look with contempt on their husbands" (v. 17b). Two decrees follow. First, Vashti is dethroned and her position will be filled by "another who is better than she" (v. 19b). Second, "'all women [throughout his kingdom] will give honor to their husbands, high and low'" (v. 20b). Letters are sent to all the royal provinces in their own languages "declaring that every man should be master in his own house" (v. 22b). Two questions come to the fore. First, why does Queen Vashti resist? Second, how should others respond when those in power intensify constraints upon the oppressed in response to resistance to oppression?

By now it is clear that hospitality for the men serves as a means for the affirmation and consolidation of monarchical and patriarchal power. Queen Vashti's refusal to be displayed as a sexual object before the king and all the men of the kingdom leads them to fear the weakening of not only the monarchical power but also loss of patriarchal power and the privilege extended through the king's power to all men throughout the kingdom. All the men quickly fear with the king that the queen's subversive act will be emulated by other women and no man will be respected as the head of his household.

## FURTHER REFLECTIONS

### *Queen Vashti as Moral Agent*

Why does Queen Vashti refuse to honor the king's request? She had to know what the outcome would be. Why risk losing her title and

*Male Power—Female Resistance*

being banished? Surely this was not the first request by the king that demeaned her as a woman. In fact, to be the queen was to be first among the harem of women who could provide sexual pleasure for the king. Queen Vashti has had enough of her life in the king's harem and she decides to resist publicly. Because Vashti chooses to resist *knowing* that there will be consequences, hers is an act of moral courage. Queen Vashti, like Orpah in Ruth, is only briefly in the story. As such, she might be considered simply a foil for Esther. However, Vashti is more than a foil, and we will miss some lessons about moral agency if we fail to acknowledge her role in the story.

First, Vashti frees herself from being the property of the king as she refuses to let her body be objectified for male pleasure. This refusal reminds us that patriarchy is a system maintained through men's power over and control of women's bodies. Examples of these patriarchal dynamics are evident in history and today. Here is a historical example. Sara Baartman, an indigenous South African Khoikhoi woman, was sold into slavery during Dutch colonization of Africa. Sara was demeaned as an enslaved person who was put on display because of her large buttocks and skin color, even being caged, barely clothed, and observed along with other animals. She was nicknamed the Hottentot Venus. By 1815 Sara was studied by scientists in France who declared her a link between animals and humans. Sara died at the age of twenty-six; her body was dissected, and one of the doctors made "a plaster cast of her body, pickled her brain and genitals and stored them in jars which were placed on display at the *Musée de l'Homme (Museum of Man)* until 1974." It took eight years after President Mandela requested her remains for them to be returned to South Africa for burial.[1]

Here is a contemporary example. In February 2019, Anjanette Young, an African American social worker, had just arrived home from work and was changing clothes when police officers authorized by a no-knock warrant broke into and raided her apartment. "Chicago police body camera video footage showed officers with guns drawn and handcuffing her while she was naked. After about two minutes, police covered Young with a blanket." Ms. Young spoke

---

1. South African History Online, "Sara 'Saartjie' Baartman," https://www.sahistory.org.za/people/sara-saartjie-baartman.

of being afraid for her life, "scared into compliance," as the officers blatantly disregarded her exposed body. It took two years for the footage to be released.[2] Ms. Young's fear was not unfounded. In March 2020, Breonna Taylor, a twenty-six-year-old African American medical services worker, was shot to death by Louisville police in her apartment. Again, police forcibly entered the apartment with a no-knock warrant because they thought her boyfriend might have been involved in criminal activity.[3]

Women who protest or resist oppressive power structures pay for it with their reputations, employment, loss of life, and abuse of their bodies. Civil rights activist Fannie Lou Hamer fought for voters' rights in Mississippi and testified before the credentials committee at the Democratic Convention in 1964. Thrown in jail for her voting rights activism, Hamer suffered physical abuse that left her permanently disabled. Hamer describes her condition after a beating in these words: "When they was (sic) finished my hands was navy blue and I was hard. I was hard like metal."[4]

One white feminist scholar suggests that Vashti and Esther represent two different models of resistance: (1) direct dissent (Vashti) and (2) working within the system (Esther). Vashti's direct confrontation reminds us that sometimes we must respond to the evils of oppression forthrightly to expose what is wrong and get the attention of others. The reformist approach alone may not always awaken others to what needs to be changed in the way that the direct approach does. The two approaches should be seen, however, as complementary rather than as contradictory. Moral agents must assess what approach is needed and when; they must be prepared to endure short-term and long-term consequences of their

---

2. Jasmine Brown, Sabina Ghebremedhin, and Haley Yamada, "Woman Whose Chicago Home Was Wrongly Raided by Police: 'I Feared for My Life,'" ABC News, December 18, 2020, https://abcnews.go.com/US/chicago-mayor-apologizes-woman-home-wrongly-raided -police/story?id=74787134.

3. Richard A. Oppel, Jr., Derrick Bryson Taylor, and Nicholas Bogel-Burroughs, "What to Know about Breonna Taylor's Death," August 23, 2024, NewYorkTimes.com, https://www.nytimes.com/article/breonna-taylor-police.html; "Breonna Taylor: What Happened on the Night of her Death? BBC, October 8, 2020, https://www.bbc.com/news /world-us-canada-54210448.

4. Margaret Parker Brooks and Davis W. Houck, eds., "Federal Trial Testimony, Oxford, Mississippi, December 2, 1963," in *The Speeches of Fannie Lou Hamer: To Tell It Like It Is* (Jackson: University Press of Mississippi, 2011), 14, Kindle.

Male Power—Female Resistance

choices. After her repeated experiences of debasement, Queen Vashti chooses direct dissent.

The moral courage of Queen Vashti pushes us to consider the roots and aims of our resistance to injustice. Is our resistance motivated by a desire for inclusion in the structures of power and privilege that already exist? Or is it motivated by a desire to discern what God's justice requires for equity and inclusion of everyone? Queen Vashti's moral courage and agency definitely strikes against the structures of power and privilege. However, her solitary action does not create movement toward systemic change; in this case, it leads to greater oppression against women as a social group. If Vashti had acted as a religious ethical mediator, she could have used her position to change conditions for the king's harem. The challenge is to act strategically in line with the overarching ethical framework of God's justice. Decision-making and action derived from such a framework guard against acting impulsively, even if the impulse is for justice. The religious ethical mediation hermeneutic insists that we ground our agency in the perspective of theocentric justice and enlarge the scope of moral community to whom we are accountable.

## Religious Ethical Mediation Interpretation

This book opens with the kind of gendered violence intrinsic to systems of class stratification and patriarchal oppression: (1) the class and gender stratification of the society and (2) the sexual objectification and legal oppression of women. Class stratification is evident as two banquets are held: one for the officials of the court and one for all men of the kingdom. This division among the men points to differences in their economic and professional statuses. Likewise, patriarchal privilege is tied to the political system controlled by the king and his allies. Although all the men of the kingdom are to be protected by the decree that "all women will give honor to their husbands, high and low alike," men of lower economic status and with less political power receive their patriarchal benefits contingent upon their willingness to put their male identity above all other interests.

During slavery, white men in the United States allowed their gender to override their class interests. White owners of slave plantations were actually a small percentage of the population; but support for the slavocracy existed across class lines because the aim was to keep Black persons enslaved because of the ideology of white supremacy.[5] More recently, there are similar dynamics of class-racial stratification and patriarchal oppression supported by a political system that privileges white racial identity, conservative politics, and wealth. For example, during the confirmation hearings for Supreme Court nominee Brett Kavanaugh, conservative legislators and pastors protested questioning him about an allegation of sexual assault in the past. Womanist ethicist Keri Day summed it up thus: "This is a privilege that is not accorded so many black boys and men. What excuses Kavanaugh from being called to account, to determine if indeed his alleged actions caused trauma in the life of a fifteen-year-old girl? Kavanaugh desires to be chosen for one of the highest positions in our nation. Why shouldn't a fair and proper investigation be conducted in light of these serious allegations?"[6] Furthermore, amid the controversy around the supreme court nominee, the president calls women liars, demeans them, and blames mainstream media as well as progressive political leaders for this "fake news." Eventually he insinuates that it is men, not women, who are under attack in society, and many white men in society seem to agree with him.[7]

In a white supremacist patriarchy, powerful white men protect and maintain their patriarchal power and privilege across all sectors of society. Recently and publicly in the United States that power and privilege is being exposed by women in the film and television

5. Jack Bloom, *Class, Race, and the Civil Rights Movement* (Bloomington: Indiana University Press, 1987), 29–30.

6. Keri Day, "White Boys Will Be Boys: Kavanaugh, #MeToo, and Race," Religion News Service, September 28, 2018, https://religionnews.com/2018/09/28/white-boys-will-be-boys-kavanaugh-metoo-and-race/; cf. The Kavanaugh confirmation hearing process is particularly interesting when compared to the confirmation hearing process for Clarence Thomas. Thomas was accused of sexual harassment by law professor Anita Hill (his former law clerk), and the charges were heard in detail before his confirmation. Kavanaugh's accuser, Professor Christine Blasey Ford, but public outrage expressed by the white male senators to hearing her accusation was very different. Importantly, both Kavanaugh and Thomas were confirmed to the court, in spite of accusations.

7. Katie Rielly, "President Trump Says His Own Sexual Misconduct Allegations Make Him Less Likely to Believe Kavanaugh Accusers," *Time*, September 26, 2018, http://time.com/5407590/doanld-trump-less-likely-to-believe-kavanaugh-accusers/.

*Male Power—Female Resistance*

industry, in government, on college campuses, and in churches. Well-known actors, directors, government leaders, and church officials have been accused of sexual harassment and rape, and some of these men are even being tried in court as women make public accusations. Despite public exposure and criminal allegations, there is a failure to believe women. White feminist theologian Susan Brooks Thistlethwaite sums this up well:

> This society, in its customs, laws, and religions, is actually held together in its current suppressive form by the capacity of some to abuse others and then have the truth of that act disbelieved.
>
> This societal glue is made up not only of the exploitation itself, but also by the widespread capacity to smother the truth about exploitation that is so necessary for this society to function the way it does. The millions of cries and even screams must be held in check or the cracks in the foundation of suppressive power would get even bigger and perhaps the whole thing could collapse.[8]

Likewise, when the right to vote was to be extended beyond white males with property and power, that extension did not include women of any race or class. There are continuing persistent legal efforts to support voter suppression, especially targeting Black and Brown voters.[9] A profile of former President Trump's base of supporters during the 2016 election reveals six groups: white evangelicals, white men, white non-college, white over fifty, white over $50,000, and white rural.[10] As in the text, different social classes in this base seem willing to collapse all of their social group and individual interests into those of the president—even given the

---

8. Dr. Susan Brooks Thistlethwaite, "The Moral Imperative of #BelievetheWomen," Patheos, September 18, 2018, https://www.patheos.com/blogs/religionnow/2018/09/the -moral-imperative-of-believethewomen-brett-kavanaugh-christine-blasey-ford/?utm _source=Newsletter&utm_medium=email&utm_campaign=Best+of+Patheos&utm _content=57.

9. Brian Duignan, "Voter Suppression," *Encyclopedia Britannica*, May 11, 2021, https://www .britannica.com/topic/voter-suppression; "Block the Vote: How Politicians Are Trying to Block Voters from the Ballot Box, ACLU, August 17, 2021, https://www.aclu.org/news /civil-liberties/block-the-vote-voter-suppression-in-2020/.

10. Sean McElwee, "Data for Politics #14: Who Is Trump's Base?," Data for Progress, August 23, 2018, https://www.dataforprogress.org/blog/2018/8/21/data-for-politics-14-who-is -trumps-base.

great socioeconomic distance between them and him—because he assures them that his political and economic agenda will make America great again. Critically, white evangelicals became captive to this way of thinking because they chose to believe in the president and his pro-life stance as the means to attain a moral course correction for the nation.

Although it is significant (even courageous) when an individual woman such as Queen Vashti stands up to the patriarchal power structure, women in solidarity against this structure is critical to overcoming oppressive systems. Today there is a movement of survivors of sexual abuse, the #MeToo movement, that represents the collective resistance of women to systemic gender violence. The #MeToo movement was initiated a decade earlier than the tweet by actress Alyssa Milano as allegations against Hollywood producer Harvey Weinstein surfaced. An African American woman, Tarana Burke, had created #MeToo in 2006; her work centered upon Black and Brown women and girl survivors of sexual violence. As the 2017 Twitter campaign went viral, Burke was afraid that the earlier mission might be erased. She later acknowledged the continuity of the Twitter campaign in these words: "The whole time I was fretting about saving my work," Burke continued. "And I didn't realize that 'my work' was happening right in front of me."[11]

The #Me Too movement reached the churches also. The response in the churches regrettably became entangled in forgiveness for the powerful pastors rather than supporting their female accusers.[12] In response to the church's response as well as to its historical silence about violence against women, evangelical women across the theological spectrum signed a statement and initiated a campaign entitled #SilenceIsNotSpiritual.[13] One of the initial editors of the statement for this campaign lists eight ways to challenge abuse: (1) disrupt with

11. Alanna Vagianos, "Tarana Burke Reflects on the MeToo Movement 1 Year After It Went Viral," HuffPost, February 4, 2019, https://www.huffpost.com/entry/tarana-burke-me-too -movement-1-year-after-it-went-viral_n_5bc4bdcbe4b0bd9ed55ca105?ncid=NEWSSTAND 0001&guccounter=1;

12. Autumn Miles, "Where Is the Church on #MeToo?" Religion News Service, August 18, 2018, https://religionnews.com/2018/01/18/where-is-the-church-on-metoo/.

13. Eliza Griswold, "Silence Is Not Spiritual: The Evangelical #MeToo Movement," *The New Yorker*, June 15, 2018, https://www.newyorker.com/news/on-religion/silence-is-not -spiritual-the-evangelical-metoo-movement.

# Male Power—Female Resistance

prayer, (2) disrupt shallow readings of Scripture, (3) disrupt flawed biblical translations, (4) disrupt skewed history, (5) disrupt male dominance, (6) disrupt the silencing of survivors, (7) disrupt porn, and (8) disrupt ignorance.[14] The violence of sexual harassment, sexual assault, and domestic violence[15] must no longer be dismissed or, in effect, sanctioned by interpreting biblical texts through patriarchal and heterosexist lenses that reinscribe gender violence as normative or by expecting the victims of such violence to forgive their transgressors without them ever truly acknowledging or repenting of the wrong that has been committed. Women as a social group are more vulnerable than heterosexual men to gender violence, and the churches must be places where the omnipresence of God's justice takes hold through partnerships between women and men.

In the context of the #MeToo movement, it is not coincidental that there was an aggressive effort to reverse the rights of women to reproductive choices. Like the king's response in the text (Esth. 1:20–22), the response to women's resistance is legislation that restricts women's rights and expands men's control over women's bodies.

> In other words, the book of Esther is about more than past history. It calls us readers to reflect and presumably act in the challenges to human dignity that confront us today.
>
> Alice Ogden Bellis, *Helpmates, Harlots, and Heroes: Women's Stories in the Hebrew Bible* (Louisville, KY: Westminster John Knox Press, 2007), 194.

The repeal of Roe is a recent example of this. The ethical challenge for us in the churches and other faith communities is to be places where dogma does not replace thoughtful theological ethical reflection upon the meaning of justice for women as well as the need to have worship and other pastoral space that supports women's grappling with the difficult reproductive choice of having an abortion, if that choice has become theirs to make.

Moreover, we in the churches must shift from a single focus on being pro-or anti-abortion to reproductive justice, thus enlarging

---

14. Mimi Haddad, "#SilenceIsNotSpiritual: 8 Ways to Disrupt Abuse," CBE International, June 13, 2024, https://www.cbeinternational.org/resource/silenceisnotspiritual-8-ways-disrupt-abuse/.

15. See Martin R. Huecker, Kevin C. King, et al, "Domestic Violence" (updated 2023 April 9) in StatPearls [Internet] for a comprehensive discussion of the topic, https://www.ncbi.nlm.nih.gov/books/NBK499891/

our understanding of what is stake for women. According to the forerunner in the reproductive justice movement, SisterSong—Women of Color Reproductive Justice (RJ) Collective, reproductive justice is defined as "the human right to maintain personal bodily autonomy, have children, not have children, and parent the children we have in safe and sustainable communities."[16] Reproductive justice is rooted in the United Nations international human rights framework, thus combining social justice and human rights. Moreover, the Reproductive Justice framework exposes the history of the reproductive abuses of women of color and their communities, such as coerced sterilization. "This makes a reproductive justice history distinct from national histories that ignore the short-term or long-term consequences for women and their communities of the slavery regime, the program of Native genocide, anti-Asian immigration restrictions, the Mexican 'repatriation,' and the colonization of the Americas, the Pacific Islands, and the Caribbean."[17]

Similarly, the Religious Community for Reproductive Choice (RCRC), an interfaith and multiracial movement of clergy and laypeople, believe: "(1) Reproductive decision-making is sacred.; (2) Reproductive freedom is religious freedom; and (3) People of faith protect the freedom to choose."[18] White feminist Christian social ethicist Rebecca Todd Peters speaks about the need to "trust women to make moral decisions about their lives" at the heart of an ethical framework that reinterprets the biblical and theological based moral obligation of women to bear children and makes an argument for abortion as a moral good. "The heart of an ethic of reproductive justice is the affirmation that women's capacity to control their fertility—whether that happens through contraception, abstinence, or abortion—is a moral good. Moral good refers to our human capacity to discern what is right and just and to act on it accordingly. For Christians, knowledge of what is morally good must be consistent with an understanding of God's justice and of

16. https://www.sistersong.net/reproductive-justice.
17. Loretta J. Ross and Rickie Solinger, *Reproductive Justice: An Introduction* (Oakland: University of California, 2017), 16, Kindle.
18. Religious Community for Reproductive Choice, https://rcrc.org/.

God's desire for humanity and for the common good."[19] It is time for the church to let go of binary pro-life and anti-abortion positions and embrace reproductive justice as the basis of our theo-ethical reflection on how to be a church that trusts women.

---

19. Rebecca Todd Peters, *Trust Women: A Progressive Christian Argument for Reproductive Justice* (Boston: Beacon, 2018), 202–3, Kindle.

# Esther 2

## 2:1–4
### *The Search for a Queen Begins*

The search for a queen begins with a search for young virgins to fill the king's harem from which he will select a queen. Commissioners are appointed in each province to gather beautiful young virgins, and the girl who pleases the king (the most beautiful and sexually appealing) will become queen. Just as King Ahasuerus issued a royal order and decree about the authority of men in their households, the search for a queen is legally mandated and managed by the appointment of commissioners in all provinces.

## 2:5–11
### *An Unlikely Prospect for Queen*

These verses introduce Mordecai and his adopted daughter, Esther. Mordecai and Esther are among the Jews exiled in the kingdom of Ahasuerus. As the king's edict is carried out, Esther is taken to the king's palace; she becomes a favorite of the king's eunuch, Hegai, who supervises the young virgins. Esther advances quickly to the best place in the harem because Hegai favors her, instructing her on what appeals to the king. Per Mordecai's instruction, Esther is to protect her family and all the Jewish people in the kingdom by not revealing that she is a Jew.

*Esther Is Chosen* **87**

# 2:12–18

## *Esther Is Chosen*

These verses reveal the process by which the young women are vetted to be queen. After twelve months of cosmetic treatments, a young woman spends a night with the king; she then becomes a member of the harem of concubines who will not visit the king again unless summoned by him. When it is Esther's turn to go to the king, she takes only what Hegai advises. Esther is chosen by the king: "the king loved Esther more than all the other women; of all the virgins she won his favor and devotion, so that he set the royal crown on her head and made her queen instead of Vashti" (v. 17). The selection of Esther is a celebration of triumph for the king and a holiday for all the provinces with the bestowing of gifts "with royal liberality" (v. 18b). Not unlike the opening banquet, this banquet is about the king's status and power and reinforcing the social and political hierarchy that sanctions male privilege to control women.

> In addition to her beauty and obedience, Esther's ascension to the throne is predicated in part on passing, allowing the dominant culture to believe she is "one of them" and enjoying the privilege that comes from being an insider.
>
> Gale A. Yee, *The Hebrew Bible: Feminist and Intersectional Perspectives* (Minneapolis: Fortress, 2018), 142.

## *Religious Ethical Mediation Interpretation*

Queen Vashti is banished for her resistance, and the monarchy and the patriarchy retain its hold as the king seeks a replacement queen among young virgin girls. Again, a new queen is chosen by King Ahasuerus based on the female's beauty and sexual ability to please the king. The king is clearly captive to a worldview in which women are objects to be beheld and controlled. And, entangled in the worldview of oppressors, the oppressed individual and/or group frequently chooses survival at whatever costs. How do we assess the demand of Mordecai that Esther keep her Jewish identity hidden? Is keeping one's identity hidden from an oppressor an act of assimilation that connotes captivity to a worldview that supports oppression? What differentiates actions necessary for survival from actions that purposively or unconsciously obstruct liberation?

Passing has been and continues to be a survival strategy for members of oppressed groups. Most often passing is assessed as a choice made by an individual for the benefit of the individual. I think that passing is a "forced" choice to ensure safety and security within a context where certain groups are denied opportunity or access to goods of society, hated because of their ethnicity or religion, or deemed less than human because they do not conform to normative gender identities or behaviors. The costs of passing include alienation from family or community, psychological distress, and self-debasement.

Dr. Allyson Hobbs, an African American historian, in her book *A Chosen Exile: A History of Racial Passing*, presents the story of Dr. Albert Johnston, a medical doctor, who passed for twenty years; he and his wife hid their Black identity from their neighbors as well as their children. During World War II, Dr. Johnston confessed his true racial identity as he was about to enter the Navy; he was rejected by the Navy and fired from the hospital where he worked. Hobbs suggests that Dr. Johnston's decision was both a personal decision and one impacted by racial perceptions of the society. In her words, "from the late eighteenth century to the present, racially ambiguous men and women have wrestled with complex questions about the racial conditions of their times, and they have fashioned complex understanding about their places in the world."[1] Today given our awareness of multiracialism and individuals who self-identify in multiracial and multiethnic terms,[2] passing may still occur because of immigration status, gender identity, or disabilities.[3] As I stated

---

1. Allyson Hobbs, *A Chosen Exile: A History of Racial Passing in American Life* (Cambridge: Harvard University, 2014), 5, Kindle.

2. Tiger Woods coined the term "Cablinasian" to signify his multiracial, multiethnic identity as Caucasian Black Indian (Native American) Asian, https://www.liveabout.com/tiger-woods-ethnicity-1566365.

3. Jeffery A. Brune and Daniel J. Wilson, introduction to *Disability and Passing: Blurring the Lines of Identity*, ed. Jeffrey A. Brune and Wilson J. Daniel (Philadelphia: Temple University Press, 2013). Disability passing is a complex and wide-ranging topic. Most often the term refers to the way people conceal social markers of impairment "to avoid the stigma of disability and pass as 'normal.'" However, it also applies to other ways people manage their identities, which can include exaggerating a condition to get some type of benefit or care. Going further,

*Esther Is Chosen* 89

above, passing is a "forced" choice because of the social prejudices and biases against certain groups in a society.

Also, this part of the Esther narrative pushes us to inquire about systems of oppression and assimilation into them. The race-gender-class system allows wealthy, powerful men to oppress women with impunity. Gendered violence is manifest through the social roles and gender scripts for women and men. Women are to be available to men and supporters of social norms that require women's obedience and submission. Men maintain structures that divide women as a social group, giving some women access to patriarchal privilege based on ideals of beauty, skin color, and stereotypes of different groups of women, or deny the humanity of others based on sexual identity.

Within faith communities we participate in these forms of gendered violence: (a) women are denied primary leadership roles as clergy based on interpretations of theological doctrines regarding women's inferiority and biblical texts about women's subordination to men, (b) LGBTQIA+ persons are not accepted as members or clergy based upon doctrines of sin, (c) gender-exclusive language for God and humankind is used in liturgy in ways that maintain a hierarchy that reflects the sociocultural gender hierarchy, and (d) biblical prooftexts ground theology that provide justifications for social myths about masculinity and femininity.

African American theologian Stephen Ray writes about "the sins of sin-talk."[4] Ray states: "My contention is that much of social sin-talk is highly problematic, because in an effort to name social sin, theologians often unwittingly describe it in terms that may themselves be profoundly racist, sexist, heterosexist, anti-Semitic, and classist."[5] In order to avoid this, theologians should pay attention to who is labelled a sinner and how that labelling is connected to the social forces of a context. He explains two sins of sin-talk. First, there is the welfare queen, a label that has been applied to Black women as sexually irresponsible women who create an aberrant matriarchy

---

disability passing encompasses the ways that others impose, intentionally or not, a specific disability or nondisability identity on a person.

4. Stephen G. Ray Jr., *Do No Harm: Social Sin and Christian Responsibility* (Minneapolis: Fortress, 2003), xiv.

5. Ibid.

in US society. This is the irresponsibility/marginalization model of sin-talk. Second, the homosexual is marked as a person who defiles the natural order. This is a defilement/essentialization model of sin-talk.[6] Thus the church must examine how its doctrine(s) of sin may force individuals to deny or closet their identities as well as support public policy that perpetrates social injustice.

Moreover, when we remember that the search for a queen is a search for young virgins, this story can open our eyes to the numbers of young girls who are victims of human trafficking today. As is the case with contemporary human trafficking, the young virgin girls are abducted. They are brought to Persia and held captive in the king's harem. They are forced to have nonconsensual sex with the king, and he will choose who pleases him most. "These elements of abduction, transportation, and captivity are all stages in the process of sex trafficking. Recognizing this process for what it is as it unfolds within the narrative exposes the inherent violence and horror of this biblical text of terror."[7]

Human trafficking is defined by the United States of Department of Justice thus:

> Human trafficking, also known as trafficking in persons, is a crime that involves compelling or coercing a person to provide labor or services, or to engage in commercial sex acts. The coercion can be subtle or overt, physical or psychological. Exploitation of a minor for commercial sex is human trafficking, regardless of whether any form of force, fraud, or coercion was used.[8]

From this perspective, Esther and the other young virgins gathered in the search for a queen may be seen as the victims of human trafficking.

Human trafficking and sexual exploitation of girls and women is primarily carried out by men, although some women have been prosecuted; it is a domestic and global human rights issue. Trafficked victims are vulnerable for many reasons, such as being a member of

---

6. Ibid., 4, 5.

7. Ericka Shawndricka Dunbar, *Trafficking Hadassah: Collective Trauma, Cultural Memory, and Identity in the Book of Esther and in the African Diaspora* (New York: Routledge, 2022), 41, Kindle.

8. U.S. Department of Justice, "What Is Human Traffkicking?" https://www.justice.gov /humantrafficking/what-is-human-trafficking.

*Esther Is Chosen*                                                                91

a minoritized social group, having undocumented status as migrants, identifying as LGBTQIA+, or being runaways or homeless, to name a few. An important myth about human traffickers that must be dispelled is that they are only hardened criminals. Frequently, those who recruit or seduce their victims have positions of authority, are known and trusted individuals, business owners, and other pillars of the community.[9]

Churches can play an important role in promoting anti-human trafficking. A first step is to accept that Christians have a duty to engage in public debate about injustices and not hide behind a misconstrued understanding of the separation of church and state. Also, a theological framework that focuses on the participation of individuals in the evil and sin of human trafficking cannot stand alone. That framework must be complemented by liberation theology's understandings of social sin and social salvation. Furthermore, liberation theology requires praxis—discipleship based upon continual commitment and engagement in the world as the basis of theological reflection. Churches engaged in anti-human trafficking must develop an advocacy program.[10] The Anglican Alliance has developed an 8P Freedom Framework (prevention, protection, participation, partnership, policy, prosecution, proof, prayer); an example of their liturgical resources follows:

### Freedom Prayer

Voice 1: On this holy ground of worship
In this sacred place of prayer
We have heard the voice of freedom
Crying "Let my people go."
All: Father/God of freedom,
Who leads us into life,
Deliver us from every evil:
And make of us
Deliverers of others.

---

9. Amy Novotney, "7 in 10 Human Trafficking Victims Are Women and Girls. What Are the Psychological Effects?," American Psychological Association, April 24, 2023, https://www.apa.org/advocacy/interpersonal-violence/trafficking-women-girls; "The Fight against Child Trafficking," Save the Children, https://www.savethechildren.org/us/charity-stories/child-trafficking-awareness#us.

10. Sandie Morgan, "How Can Churches Fight Human Trafficking in Their Own Backyards: Three Steps toward a More Effective Anti-trafficking Ministry," *Influence Magazine*, January

Voice 2: **Where chains restrain God's chosen children,**
**Where humans trade in kin and skin,**
**May our words pass on your promise,**
**Of a land where liberty is sweet.**
**All: Father/God of freedom,**
**Who leads us into life,**
**Deliver us from every evil:**
**And make of us**
**Deliverers of others.**
Voice 3: Give us faith to face the Pharaohs,
Who line their pockets from this plague.
Send us as salvation's sponsors,
Willing servants; slaves to love.
All: Father/God of freedom,
Who leads us into life,
Deliver us from every evil:
And make of us
Deliverers of others.
**Amen**[11]

## 2:19–23

### *A Plot against the King*

As the celebration of Esther as queen is underway, two of the king's eunuchs are plotting to kill the king. Mordecai learns of this plot while sitting at the king's gate; he tells Esther, and she reports this information to the king on behalf of Mordecai. The plot is verified, and the two men are hanged. This foiled plot is recorded in the official records of the kingdom in the presence of the king.

### *Religious Ethical Mediation Interpretation*

Amid celebration of Esther's selection as queen, there is a plot to kill the king. The plot against the king is instigated by angry eunuchs,

22, 2016, https://influencemagazine.com/Practice/How-Churches-Can-Fight-Human-Trafficking-and-Slavery-in-Their-Own-Backyards.

11. Anglican Alliance, "How Can Churches Respond to Human Trafficking?" https://anglicanalliance.org/how-can-churches-respond-to-human-trafficking/.

A Plot against the King

Bigthan and Teresh, who served the king, and Mordecai and Esther inform the king (vv. 21–22). There is no clear reason given for the eunuchs' murder plot; perhaps their position of inferiority and servitude within the court is a contributing factor. According to a queer biblical interpretation, "[Eunuchs] are 'perfect servants' to the plot of the story. In Chapter 1 seven eunuchs are named (Mehuman, Biztha, Harbona, Bigtha, Abagtha, Zethar, and Carkas). They function as go–betweens in the battle of the sexes that dominates the opening scenes of the story."[12] Eunuchs are the persons in the story who cross gender, power, and physical boundaries of the king's gate, threshold, and presence. Significantly, as carriers of messages and decrees, they cross information boundaries too. Perhaps the eunuchs who plot to kill the king are fed up with being used by the system.

The fact that these persons, the eunuchs and Mordecai and Esther, are on the margins of the power structure should not be overlooked. The dynamics of oppressor-oppressed and oppressed-oppressed relations are complex. Sometimes the oppressed choose to challenge the oppressor, as an individual or as a group, at any cost for the sake of liberation. Other times oppressed individuals and groups choose survival at whatever costs. Thus far in this story, we have seen an individual (Vashti) and a group (two eunuchs) challenge the oppressor and suffer severe consequences, banishment, and death, respectively. Meanwhile, Mordecai and Esther have chosen a strategy of survival that includes passing as well as sacrificing another oppressed group. This is not to condone the eunuchs' plot to murder the king, but minoritized groups embedded in systemic oppression become implicated in its dynamics of divide and conquer as the groups compete for survival rather than become allies against their oppressors. In fact, the structure of oppressive systems often creates a pecking order among oppressed groups.

As churches continue to be contexts where the religio-political polarization on issues of discrimination can be either fostered or discouraged, pastors of churches need to examine whether they are creating a congregational context of competitive survival among individuals and groups for resources, such as money, recognition,

12. Mona West, "Esther," in *The Queer Bible Commentary*, ed. Deryn Guest, Robert E. Goss, Mona West, and Thomas Bohache (London: SCM, 2006), 300.

or inclusion. Most often the church is a microcosm of the society's patriarchy, heteropatriarchy, heterosexism, ableism, classism, and white supremacy wherein gender, gender identity, race, ethnicity, and physical and mental ability are the bases of a pecking order of social groups. Likewise, even when churches seem homogeneous in terms of race, ethnicity, and/or social class, some persons or groups are treated as subordinate to others. Pastors must consider what their model of leadership says about who's seen and included, because of how they use their power.

In a hierarchal model of leadership, like that of King Ahasuerus, power is concentrated at the top and everyone serves the interests of the leader. In a web model of leadership, power is shared and creates a relationship between the leader at the center and those on the margins:

> Relational power is shared power. The web creates enduring and strong networks that balance the power in the organization. The leader creates an alternate center of power, usually outside the leader who is at the center of the web. This alternate power, however, is not a threat to the leader at the center but a powerful tentacle of the leader at the center's power. Like the engine within the automobile, this kind of relational and shared power takes you somewhere. If we continue to lead the church in the ways that we have during the twentieth century, we might never get there.[13]

In a church where power is relational, members become a web of interconnected relationships led by a pastor driven by a church's mission and not her or his own agenda. Theologically, the Spirit is the center of the church where web leadership is exercised.

While the national government is promoting bills to address LGBTQIA+rights in society and the military, churches continue to grapple with full inclusion of the LGBTQIA+ community.[14] The

13. Susan Hilllauck and Jacqulyn Thorpe, *The Web of Women's Leadership: Recasting Congregational Leadership* (Nashville: Abingdon, 2001), 35–36.
14. *FACT SHEET: The Biden-Harris Administration Champions LGBTQ+ Equality and Marks Pride Month*, https://www.whitehouse.gov/briefing-room/statements-releases /2021/06/01/fact-sheet-the-biden-harris-administration-champions-lgbtq-equality-and -marks-pride-month/; Sharita Gruberg, Lindsay Mahowald, and John Halpin, *The State of the LGBQT Community in 2020: A National Public Opinion Study*, The Center for American

United Methodist denomination, a Protestant mainline denomination, has been a recent example of religious debate over inclusion, and it is threatened with schism over this matter. A plan dated December 19, 2019, offered ways for those churches that were more traditionalist to withdraw with beneficial financial arrangements for ministers and regarding church properties.[15] When the General Conference convened in 2024, the denomination voted to remove discriminatory language regarding LGBTQIA+ persons from the Book of Discipline, removed the same-sex wedding ban, and adopted a regionalization plan that allows more context-dependent and culturally sensitive interpretation of these approved changes.[16] Also, Pope Francis authorized the blessing of same-sex civil unions but has not reversed the Catholic Church's position on homosexuality. The Vatican also released a statement on the inclusion of transgender persons in the sacraments.[17] As these actions indicate, the churches continue to be of divided mind. Queer theologian Patrick S. Cheng has critiqued the church in this regard as a failure of radical love. In his words: "Radical love, I contend, is *a love so extreme that it dissolves our existing boundaries*(author's emphasis), whether they are boundaries that separate us from other people, that separate us from preconceived notions of sexuality and gender identity, or that separate us from God."[18] We must consider which members, by virtue of their sexuality and gender identities, are not experiencing the church as a place of radical love. Is there a pecking order of marginalized groups in your congregation? Whose interests are being served by you as pastor, and consequently by your congregants?

Progress, October 6, 2020, https://www.americanprogress.org/issues/lgbtq -rights/reports/2020/10/06/491052/state-lgbtq-community-2020

15. Meg Anderson, United Methodist Church Announces Proposal to Split over Gay Marriage, NPR, January 4, 2020, https://www.npr.org/2020/01/04/793614135/united-methodist -church-announces-proposal-to-split-over-gay-marriage.

16. UM News, "General Conference News and Commentary," https://www.umnews.org/en /landing-pages/general-conference-news-and-commentary; Heather Han, "All That General Conference Passed," UM News, June 25, 2024, https://www.umnews.org/en/news/all-that -general-conference-passed.

17. Nicole Hassenstab, "The Vatican, LGBT Rights, and the Anti-gender Movement," January 26, 2024, https://www.american.edu/sis/news/20240126-the-vatican-lgbt-rights-and-the -anti-gender-movement.cfm.

18. Patrick S. Cheng, *Radical Love: An Introduction to Queer* (New York: Seabury, 2011), Kindle, loc. 99 of 5009.

# Esther 3

## 3:1–6

### *Roots of a Plot against the Jews*

Following the plot against the king, King Ahasuerus promotes Haman to the highest position among the king's servants. Due to his new status and the king's order, everyone is to bow before Haman. Mordecai refuses to bow down. The king's servants implored Mordecai to obey the king's order. When Mordecai continued to refuse, they informed Haman that he was a Jew. Haman is infuriated by Mordecai's refusal, but he decides not to punish Mordecai as an individual. In the words of the text: "So, having been told who Mordecai's people were, Haman plotted to destroy all the Jews, the people of Mordecai, throughout the whole kingdom of Ahasuerus" (v. 6b).

## 3:7–11

### *Haman Sets the Plot in Motion*

Haman informs King Ahasuerus that there is a people scattered throughout his kingdom who do not obey the king's laws; in fact they have their own laws. Claiming to protect the king's honor, Haman initiates an economic plan to fund a campaign against these people. King Ahasuerus signs off on this plan: "So the king took his signet ring from his hand and gave it to Haman son of Hammedatha the Agagite, the enemy of the Jews. The king said to Haman, 'The money is given to you, and the people as well, to do with them as it seems good to you'" (vv. 10–11).

*A Decree to Annihilate the Jews*  **97**

# 3:12–15

## *A Decree to Annihilate the Jews*

Under the seal of the king, an edict is issued by Haman and letters were sent to all the provinces, "giving orders to destroy, to kill, and to annihilate all Jews, young and old, women and children, in one month, which is the month of Adar, and to plunder their goods" (v. 13). The edict is issued as a decree in the provinces and in the citadel of Susa; all the peoples of the provinces are commanded to be ready. But, as the king and Haman prepared to drink to what is to come, the city of Susa "was thrown into confusion" (v. 15b).

### *Religious Ethical Mediation Interpretation*

This chapter expounds another violent reactionary response of someone in power when he feels threatened. This time it is Haman who is reacting to Mordecai's refusal to bow down before him. Haman then plots revenge against the Jewish people, not solely Mordecai. Although Haman is clearly part of the power structure, why does he feel threatened by the insubordination of one individual, or is there something more going on?

The text states that Haman is son of Hammedatha the Agagite and that Mordecai is a Benjaminite, and there is historical animosity between these families (see 1 Sam. 15). Haman's reaction to punish all the Jews may reflect this. African American Hebrew Bible scholar Randall C. Bailey agrees that this is a first sign of ethnic conflict in the narrative. Bailey notes that the guests to the royal banquet reflect that the empire has a multiethnic population. However, laws are issued that require total compliance to patriarchy (Esth. 1:20–22) and sanction genocidal acts (Esth. 3:8), ethnic group practices are tolerated. When Mordecai does not bow down to Haman, his act transgresses a law governing everyone in the empire.[1] Bailey further notes that it is ethnicity in terms of customs and practices, not

---

1. Randall C. Bailey, "That's Why They Didn't Call the Book Hadassah! The Interse(ct)/(x) ionality of Race/Ethnicity, Gender, and Sexuality in the Book of Esther," in *They Were All in One Place? Toward Minority Biblical Criticism* (Atlanta: Society of Biblical Literature, 2009), 229–31.

physical appearance, that makes it possible for Esther to hide her identity.[2]

The encounter between Haman and Mordecai points to the roots of intractable conflict between groups and how it can play out interpersonally. Intractable conflict refers to conflict that "seems to elude resolution;" terms such as protracted, deep-rooted, complex, and enduring signify this type of conflict.[3] Race relations in the United States and the Palestinian-Israeli conflict are examples of this type of intractable conflict.

Race relations in the United States is intractable conflict because there is a history of racial terror that undergirds the Black Lives Matter movement in the twenty-first century. In the report *Lynching in America: Confronting the Legacy of Racial Terror*, the Equal Justice Initiative documents 4,075 "racial terror lynchings" in twelve southern states between 1877 and 1950. Moreover, "the report explores the ways in which lynching profoundly impacted race relations in this country and shaped the contemporary geographic, political, social, and economic conditions of African Americans."[4]

Likewise, the rise in Asian hate incidents and crimes during the recent COVID-19 pandemic has historical roots, such as Chinese Americans being blamed for diseases such as malaria and cholera during the nineteenth century, the exploitation of Chinese workers in the building of our first transcontinental railroad, and the internment of Japanese Americans in detention camps during World War II. The impact of anti-Asian violence upon the Asian, Asian American, and Pacific Islander (AAPI) community has long-term psychological and economic impacts as fear increases and individuals are fired from their jobs.[5] A video of some comments made to Asian

2. Ibid.

3. Heidi Burgess and Guy M, Burgess, "What Are Intractable Conflicts?" Beyond Intractability, November 2003, https://www.beyondintractability.org/essay/meaning_intractability#masthead.

4. "Lynching in America: Confronting the Legacy of Racial Terror," Equal Justice Initiative, https://eji.org/reports/lynching-in-america/?gclid=Cj0KCQjw5uWGBhCTARIsAL70sLLg ofn-eC1G90pAxqRdjHEdiuh8eiTMdefxbFPazfwNCu28pOW2sH4aAlvXEALw_wcB; Black Lives Matter, https://www.blacklivesmatter.com/

5. Carmen Reinicke, "How the Pandemic and a Rise in Targeted Hate Crimes Has Shifted Spending for Asian Americans," NBC News, June 2, 2021, https://www.nbcnews.com/news/asian-america/pandemic-rise-targeted-hate-crimes-shifted-spending-asian-americans -rcna1097; Elizabeth Lee, "Anti-Asian Hate in US Predates Pandemic," Voice of America, May

American and Pacific Islander clergy and lay leaders at church meetings demonstrate how historical roots of discrimination show up in interpersonal relationships; here is a sample of comments from the video:

> "Can you speak English?"
> "What a nice suit. Now you look like an American."
> "If you want to do ministry, why don't you do it in your own country?"
> "You speak English so well."[6]

We in the churches must be more aware of unconscious bias that feeds racist comments that become the basis of intractable conflict within our congregations. At the same time, we must not forget that conflict does not have to become intractable. Energies of conflict are present within all contexts; we can shift these in a positive or negative direction by the choices that we make. Living as a religious ethical mediator, we respond to conflict in concert with the energy of God during Creation and the leading of the Holy Spirit.

---

26, 2021, https://www.voanews.com/a/usa_anti-asian-hate-us-predates-pandemic/6206218.html.

6. "Dismantling Racism: Asian American Pacific Islander," United Methodist Videos, YouTube, https://www.youtube.com/watch?v=qepo3t3hbKc.

# Esther 4

## 4:1–3

### *Mordecai Laments*

Mordecai hears of the orders to annihilate all Jews. He tears his clothes off and puts on sackcloth and ashes. He proceeds through the streets of the city, "wailing with a loud and bitter cry" (v. 1b), ending up at the entrance to the palace. Meanwhile, because of the king's orders and decree in all the provinces, "there was great mourning among the Jews with fasting and weeping and lamenting, and most of them lay in sackcloth and ashes" (v. 3b).

## 4:4–8

### *Esther Learns of Mordecai's Condition*

Esther's maids and eunuchs inform Esther of Mordecai's grievous condition. Esther sends clothes to her uncle to replace his sackcloth; Mordecai refuses them. Mordecai's refusal of the clothes distresses Esther, and she sends the king's eunuch Hathach to talk with Mordecai. Mordecai tells Hathach about Haman's plan: "and Mordecai told him all that had happened to him, and the exact sum of money that Haman had promised to pay in the king's treasuries for the destruction of the Jews" (v. 7). Mordecai gives Hathach a copy of the "written decree issued in Susa for their destruction that he might show it to Esther, explain it to her, and charge her to go to the king to make supplication to him and entreat him for her people" (v. 8).

Esther's Decision 101

# 4:9–17

## *Esther's Decision*

Hathach relays Mordecai's message and instruction to Esther. Esther sends a return message via Hathach. Her message reminds Mordecai of the protocol for going before the king; if anyone enters the inner court without being summoned by the king, the sentence is death. There is one way to avoid the death sentence; the king holds out the golden scepter and the person lives. Furthermore, Esther had not been summoned by the king for thirty days. This information was relayed to Mordecai. Mordecai sends a return message: "Do not think that in the king's palace you will escape any more than all the other Jews. For if you keep silence at such a time as this, relief and deliverance will rise for the Jews from another quarter, but you and your father's family will perish. Who knows? Perhaps you have come to royal dignity for just such a time as this" (vv. 13–15). Esther makes a counterresponse in which she calls upon all the Jews in Susa to hold a fast on her behalf for three days, and she and her maids will do the same. The crux of the message is this: "After that I will go to the king, though it is against the law; and if I perish, I perish" (v. 16b). Mordecai received and followed the instructions of Esther's message.

## *Religious Ethical Mediation Interpretation*

Mordecai's disobedience/insubordination sets a chain of events in motion that leads to a decree calling for the annihilation of the Jewish people. Here again the response of the powerful (Haman) is reactionary and comprehensive. Vashti is punished, but so are all women (cf. 1:19–20). Mordecai is the offending party, but it is all Jewish people who will be punished. Why does the punishment of a minoritized individual have collective consequences whereas individuals of oppressor groups tend to be punished as individual offenders?

The response on behalf of the Jewish people is now being guided by Esther. Mordecai offers a directive to Esther, reminding her of her duty to save her people and the responsibility of her royal position (v. 14b). Importantly, though, Esther takes control of the situation by calling for a collective fast on her behalf in preparation to go before the king. Given what happened to the insubordinate Queen Vashti, we readers must now contemplate Esther's fate. Will Esther be able to persuade the king not to allow the mass murder of her people? Under what condition(s) does the oppressor move from tolerating to respecting the humanity of the oppressed?

Mordecai and Haman are entangled in a conflict spiral. Mordecai is rebelling against the system that Haman represents, and Haman is using the power of that system to constrain rebellion. Haman and Mordecai have both been socialized to see one another as the enemy. As stated earlier, seeing one another as an enemy may have specific historical roots. But, whether those roots exist or not, Haman and Mordecai are embedded in a system that requires enemies or scapegoats. First, Haman is Mordecai's enemy: he has the power to control Mordecai's fate as well as that of his community. Second, Mordecai is Haman's enemy: he threatens Haman's status and power. Third, both men are competing for a place in the monarchy that befits men in a patriarchy. Last, they are both, in effect, pawns of the monarchy, and eventually one of them, Haman, becomes a scapegoat that ensures the stability of the monarchy (see 7:3–10).

We must ask how we become pawns in oppressive systems that require scapegoats.[1] Violence against the Asian American Pacific Islander (AAPI) community during the COVID pandemic derived from President Trump's repeated emphasis that this was a Chinese virus. The president used this claim about the virus to shift attention away from critiques about his leadership during this time of crisis. Without clear evidence to support the claim, members of racial ethnic groups, including racial ethnic groups of color, across the country made the AAPI community a scapegoat for the pandemic.[2] The

---

1. "Scapegoat Theory," *Psychology*, https://psychology.iresearchnet.com/social-psychology /social-psychology-theories/scapegoat-theory/. Neel Burton, "The Psychology of Scapegoating: Is the Time Ripe for a New Wave of Scapegoating?" *Psychology Today*, June 22, 2024, https://www.psychologytoday.com/us/blog/hide-and-seek/201312/the-psychology -of-scapegoating.
2. Kimmy Yam, "Viral Images Show People of Color as Anti-Asian Perpertrators. That Misses the Big Picture," NBC News, June 15, 2021, https://www.nbcnews.com/news/asian-america /viral-images-show-people-color-anti-asian-perpetrators-misses-big-n1270821.

*Esther's Decision*

violence against Asian Americans by another minoritized group such as African Americans is illustrative. Nadia Kim, professor of sociology and Asian American studies at Loyola Marymount University, speaks about this situation thus: "It is violence—especially for a group that has been de-racialized and basically whitened."[3] Having been stereotyped as the "model minority" by whites, the achievements of Asian Americans offered proof that the United States is a land of equal opportunity and meritocracy works. Meanwhile, African Americans accepted the model minority myth about Asian Americans, a myth of the white supremacist patriarchal system of discrimination driven by a Black-white racial binary. Thus, it is not surprising when African Americans become pawns of the racist system. The idea that individuals and groups can be pawns of a system does not mean that they should not be held accountable for the harm done to others. The point here is to stress the interrelatedness of interpersonal and systemic violence. The challenge is to examine and reconstruct (if needed) denominational or local church policies that discriminate against individuals and groups, uncovering their roots in historical relationships between groups as well as stereotypes and myths about social groups.

---

3. Kimmy Yam, "How Hate Incidents Led to a Reckoning Causal Racism against Asian Americans, NBC News, June 23, 2021, https://www.nbcnews.com/news/asian-america/how-hate-incidents-led-reckoning-casual-racism-against-asian-americans-n1271729.

# Esther 5

## 5:1–8

### *Esther Extends an Invitation to the King*

After the three days of fasting, Esther donned her royal robes and entered the inner court of the king's palace outside the king's hall. When the king sees Esther, he is enthralled and extends the golden scepter. Esther touches the top of the scepter and is invited in by the king. The king asks her what she desires, even up to half of his kingdom. Esther invites the king and Haman to a banquet; the king agrees eagerly. At the banquet, the king asks Esther again what she desires. In response Esther invites Haman and the king to another banquet, thinking if she still has his favor, then she will reveal her identity as she pleads for the life of her people.

## 5:9–14

### *Haman's Pride and Plot*

Haman has just attended a banquet to which he and the king are the only ones who have been invited. Haman feels honored until he encounters Mordecai at the king's gate. Mordecai does not rise to show Haman honor and respect, and Haman becomes infuriated. Haman calls for his friends and his wife to tell them about Mordecai's affront to all that he is and has: "Haman recounted to them the splendor of his riches, the number of his sons, all the promotions with which the king had honored him, and how he had advanced above the officials and ministers of the king" (v. 11). Zeresh, his wife, and his friends advise Haman to build gallows and have Mordecai hanged; Haman concurs, and the gallows are constructed.

## Religious Ethical Mediation Interpretation

Believing she now has the collective strength of the Jewish people behind her, Esther requests an audience with the king. The king receives her; she invites the king and Haman to a banquet. Following what was apparently a successful banquet because the king asks Esther again what she desires, Esther invites them to another banquet. As Haman leaves the banquet, he encounters Mordecai, who fails to show him the legally required respect of bowing to him. There are several questions to consider: Why does Esther construct such an elaborate plan to make her request of the king? Why not be straightforward and make the request immediately when the king grants her permission to address him? Are Esther's actions strategic or manipulative? Does it matter when acting under conditions of oppression?

Esther's behavior must be interpreted considering her social location. Esther uses strategic reasoning from her "outsider/within marginal location"; "such outsider/within marginal locations provide one with the unique opportunity to demystify and demythologize the conundrums of domination."[1] Also, from this location Esther knows that she is accountable to her community and not to those in power.[2]

Esther begins her strategic plan; she will manipulate King Ahasuerus and Haman to accomplish the larger aim of saving the Jewish people. Esther has been in the palace long enough to know that she must play to the king's ego. The first banquet was most likely to assure the king of her admiration for and loyalty to him, further securing his commitment to her. The second banquet is to create a context wherein the king will accept that Haman is at the center of the genocidal plot against the Jewish community. Interestingly, the way that Haman is exposed also aligns with the need to stroke the king's ego. When the king catches Haman in a compromising position with Queen Esther, his personal affront guides his political

---

1. Kelly Brown Douglas, "Marginalized People, Liberating Perspectives: A Womanist Approach to Biblical Interpretation," in *I Found God in Me: A Womanist Biblical Hermeneutics Reader*, ed. Mitzi J. Smith (Eugene, OR: Cascade, 2015), 82.

2. Ibid.

response, as was the case when he legalized patriarchal control of women in response to Vashti's rebuff.

Pastors can be manipulated by members using social and political causes that they support. This support engenders loyalty to the pastor (meets his or her ego need). It is probably not the intent of members to manipulate the pastor or undermine commitment to a larger vision of the church's mission. However, churches are populated by humans, and humans have needs, desires, and interests that undermine a common good. When needs, desires, and interests of humans collide with a collective mission of the church, we need to understand more about how to encounter one another faithfully in the church as a site of conflict. Each of us must pray about how our own intrapersonal conflict may contribute to how we engage interpersonal conflict. Also, conflict in church may be over beliefs, issues, values, goals, or means. As stated above, if congregational leadership is weblike, the pastor exercises relational power and the Spirit is the center of the church; conflict will then be engaged constructively through collaboration[3] and other practices consistent with religious ethical mediation. Practicing religious ethical mediation values process over finding *a single* solution or *a preconceived* end.

## FURTHER REFLECTIONS
### *Esther as Moral Agent*

Much scholarly literature has been written in the last couple of decades about the book of Esther and about who Esther is as a character in the story. In this section I will share some of those intriguing scholarly interpretations. Some think of Esther as a symbol for exiled Jewish people who are under threat. She advocates for the Jewish people from her position as a "quadruply disadvantaged individual—a woman, an orphan, a Jew, and a captive in the king's court."[4] Still, although Mordecai informs Esther of the impending

---

3. This discussion derives from my reading of Norma Cook Everist, *Church Conflict: From Contention to Collaboration* (Nashville: Abingdon, 2004).

4. Sylvia Barack Fishman, "Reading Esther: Cultural Impact on Responses to Biblical Heroines" (working paper, Hadassah International Research Institute on Jewish Women at Brandeis University Working Paper, February 2002), 10.

*Haman's Pride and Plot*                                            **107**

threat to the Jewish people, Esther strategizes how to engage the threat; she calls for a fast of the people and determines the best way to approach the king.

The book of Esther is characterized by "conceptual metaphors of the self" that "speak to questions of subjective agency."[5] These metaphors are consistent with the Deuteronomic conceptualization in the Hebrew Bible of the self as "heart" where the moral will resides. One theme of these metaphors is obedience and disobedience (e.g., Esther obeys Mordecai in chapter 2; Mordecai obeys Esther in chapter 4; Vashti does not comply with the king's request in chapter 1; Mordecai does not bow down to Haman in chapter 3), and actions related to obedience and disobedience may or may not be moral choices. However, in the book of Esther, these metaphors also demonstrate how characters "disavow agency, conceiving the self as easily manipulated and unsettled by external forces,"[6] as is especially the case with King Ahasuerus and Haman.

In contrast, the subjectivity of Esther's self is earmarked by disclosure and nondisclosure. Indeed, Esther is both same and other, "us" and "them." Her mutually incompatible, "socially impossible" selves exceed any single location within the social order that has been established, and her strategic self-revelation destabilizes formerly stable relations, unsettling both Haman's and the king's selves. Not that Esther had been *hiding* her various socially incompatible identities. Rather, she is in control and chooses when and how to reveal them. Self-control is thus linked here to the self's inaccessibility.[7] Esther as a moral agent must be evaluated from the perspective of living under threat as the consummate insider-outsider.

Using ritual theory as a lens to interpret Esther 2:12–14, Esther and the other young virgins undergo a shift from "girlhood to concubine." Following a series of cosmetic treatments and sexual encounters that function like rites of passage, these young girls cut previous social ties and are prepared for a new status, their life in the "royal harem." As "royal concubines" they are expected to be

---

5. Timothy Beal, "'Who Filled His Heart to Do This?' Conceptual Metaphors of the Self in the Book of Esther," *Journal of the Study of the Old Testament*, 40.1 (2015): 97.
6. Ibid., 105.
7. Ibid., 110.

passive and obedient, as was consistent with Mordecai's directive to Esther to not reveal her identity as a Jew.[8] Mordecai's instruction to Esther to keep her Jewish identity secret leads us to consider the next feature that impacts her moral agency, "an adaptation strategy fitted to the realities of her situatedness."[9]

Another lens for understanding Esther's behavior is that of the African trickster tradition. Old Testament scholar Madipoane Masenya (Ngwan'a Mphahlele) rereads a Northern Sotho folktale in which a hare is the trickster alongside chapter 4 in the book of Esther. Esther is considered small and powerless in relation to the king (as the hare is in relation to the lion in the tale). Likewise, the lion is an old lion who is powerful because of his position but is manipulated by his subjects; there is also a snake in this tale who embodies evil like Haman. The moral of the African tale and of Esther is this: "One should not despise those who appear small or powerless, for through their survival tactics they may take control."[10]

Also, as stated at the outset, the story of Esther is one filled with moral ambiguity. Esther uses deception as a mediator; "the trickster-mediator understands that conflict has the potential to be the source of both risk and opportunity."[11] From the perspective of this mediator theory, deception per se should not be judged pejoratively. The intention and purpose of using deception is critical.[12] Esther's intention and purpose is to save the Jewish people; thus, the means justifies the end.

Esther grows into the fullness of her moral agency during chapter 4 when she is confronted with the choice to intervene on behalf of the Jewish people. She does not immediately honor Mordecai's

---

8. On concubines as expected to be passive and obedient, see Anne-Mareike Wetter, "In Unexpected Places: Ritual and Religious Belonging in the Book of Esther," *Journal for the Study of the Old Testament* 36, no 3 (2012): 322–26.

9. Joshua A. Berman, "Hadassah Bat Abihail: The Evolution from Object to Subject in the Character of Esther," *Journal of Biblical Literature* 120/4 (2001): 649.

10. Madipoane Masenya (Ngwan'a Mphahlele), "Esther and Northern Sotho Stories: An African-South African Woman's Commentary," in *Other Ways of Reading: African Women and the Bible*, ed. Musa W. Dube (Atlanta: Society of Biblical Literature, 2001), 46.

11. Robert D. Benjamin, "Managing the Natural Energy of Conflict: Mediators, Tricksters, and the Constructive Uses of Deception," in *Bringing Peace into the Room: How the Personal Qualities of the Mediator Impact the Process of Conflict Resolution*, ed. Daniel Bowling and David Hoffman (San Francisco: Jossey-Bass, 2003), 95.

12. Ibid., 125–27.

*Haman's Pride and Plot*                                                    **109**

request to plead with the king for her people. Esther must transgress the law and can die if she goes to see the king without being summoned by him (4:11). Having concealed her Jewish identity for six years, it is no surprise that Esther is torn between personal safety and the greater good of her people. She struggles because she has lived in isolation as well as with the fear of being exposed as Jewish. Esther asks that the Jews in Susa fast on her behalf as she will do before she goes before the king. It is not Mordecai's threat (vv. 13–14) that leads Esther to say, "After that I will go to the king, though it is against the law; and if I perish, I perish" (v. 16). Instead Esther chooses to take time to discern how to approach this moral dilemma. Finally, with a strategy in mind for encountering the king, Esther puts on her royal robes and enters the inner court, hoping that the specter will be extended to her. Although Esther does not confront those in power with a direct protest like that of Queen Vashti, she does effectively undermine the system, particularly as represented by the king and Haman as we will see in chapters 5–7. Esther thus begins her role as a transformative mediator/reconciler.

Esther's decision to act on behalf of her people ("if I perish, I perish") is deliberative and exhibits the kind of intentionality that is an earmark of moral agency. Let us consider a contemporary act of moral agency by a teenager. On May 25, 2020, Darnella Frazier, a

> **Esther's plan would not be conceivable without Vashti's refusal. The prevailing sexist balance of power has been made public by Vashti's resistance and makes an analysis possible. There is a power hidden in Vashti's broken-off story that is available to Esther when she fights for survival of her people within the given structures.**
>
> Klara Butting, "Esther: A New Interpretation of the Joseph Story in the Fight against Anti-Semitism and Sexism" in *Ruth and Esther*, ed. Athalya Brenner (Sheffield: Sheffield Academic, 1999), 246.

seventeen-year-old African American teenager, used her cell phone to record the murder of George Floyd by police. As police officer Derek Chauvin pinned Mr. Floyd to the ground with his knee on his neck, Ms. Frazier filmed and published on social media the violent death of this man who exclaimed during the ordeal that he could not breathe. An excerpt of her testimony in court follows:

110 ESTHER 5:9–14

I heard George Floyd saying, I can't breathe, please, get off me. I can't breathe. He cried for his mom. He was in pain. It seemed like he knew it was over for him. He was terrified. This was a cry for help.

When I look at George Floyd, I look at my dad. I look at my brothers. I look at my cousins, my uncles, because they are all black. I have a black father. I have a black brother. I have black friends. And I look at that and I look at how that could have been one of them.[13]

Furthermore, Darnella Frazier made an intentional choice to record and post the video of this injustice; in her words: "It wasn't right. He was suffering. He was in pain," Frazier said in her testimony during the Chauvin trial. "I knew it was wrong. We all knew it was wrong."[14] Because Darnella chooses to record the event, she challenges the authority of these police to commit state-sanctioned murder. Given what she is witnessing, she could not be certain about how the police might react to what she was doing. Although Ms. Frazier speculates about whether she or other bystanders could have done more to help George Floyd, her video record played a significant part in the national and global protests that followed. The impact of her action certainly dispels the idea that she did not do enough. Likewise, Esther acts on behalf of her people because she is making space for justice to prevail.

> **The book of Esther is about more than past history. It calls its readers to reflect and presumably act in the challenges to human dignity that confront us today.**
>
> Alice Ogden Bellis, *Helpmates, Harlots, and Heroes: Women's Stories in the Hebrew Bible* (Louisville, KY: Westminster John Knox Press, 2007), 194.

Finally, sometimes individuals do not intervene in situations such as those faced by Esther and Darnella Frazier. This failure to intervene may be characterized as the action of a bystander or moral apathy. Elisabeth T. Vasko argues that bystanders can be a critical location for theological reflection: "*Bystanders* are those who aid and abet perpetrators (oppressors) through acts of 'omission

---

13. "Transcript: The ReidOut, 3/30/31," MSNBC, https://www.msnbc.com/transcripts /transcript-reidout-3-30-31-n1262587. The ReidOut is a national political news show hosted by Joy Reid on MSNBC.
14. Ibid.

*Haman's Pride and Plot*

and commission.' While bystanders can occupy a range of social locations from margin to center, many occupy social sites of privilege to some degree." She is concerned with how "a group of well-intentioned, and sometimes socially aware, individuals repeatedly bypass opportunities for resisting violence."[15] Her contention is this:

> Theology has played a role in the social conditioning of privileged apathy. In particular, I will argue that models of redemption wherein divine justice is accomplished by means of penal substitution affirm patterns of relationality undergirding white supremacy and heteropatriarchy in the United States today, erasing them from the consciousness of dominant elites. When paired within individualized notions of sin-talk, such theological language works to further privilege apathy. As such, new ways of speaking about sin and redeeming grace are sorely needed.[16]

In sum, Vasko proposes a "soteriological praxis for bystanders."[17] This praxis requires the privileged to engage in authentic solidarity with those who are oppressed. She engages the work of mujerista theologian Ada María Isasi-Díaz who asserts that solidarity is the sine qua non of salvation, "responsible relationships that are born of compassionate commitment to the liberation and full flourishing of all. In practice such a vision requires that there is a real understanding of the 'interconnections between oppression and privilege, between the rich and the poor, the oppressed and the oppressors."[18] At this point in the story, Esther and her community are clearly those who are oppressed, and she needs to ensure that her relationship with the king will lead to compassion and justice for (if not solidarity with) her people.

---

15. Elisabeth T. Vasko, *Beyond Apathy: A Theology for Bystanders* (Minneapolis: Fortress, 2015), 7, 9.
16. Ibid., 10.
17. Ibid., chap. 5.
18. Ibid., 203.

# Esther 6

## 6:1–5
### *The King Ponders How to Honor Mordecai*

During a restless night, the king is being read to by servants from the official records of his court. This reading reminds the king of how Mordecai had saved him from an assassination attempt. The king thus queries about whether Mordecai has been honored, and if not, how he should be.

## 6:6–9
### *The Kings Takes Haman's Advice*

Amid this pondering, Haman enters the king's court and is invited in by the king. The king now asks Haman about an appropriate way to honor someone. In his conceit, Haman thinks that the king can only be thinking of honoring him. So Haman elaborates an honor that consists of royal robes and a crown that had belonged to the king as well as a parade through the square led by one of the king's noble officials. The king's official shall proclaim: "Thus shall it be done for the man whom the king wishes to honor" (v. 9c).

## 6:10–14
### *Mordecai, Not Haman, Is Honored*

The king then asks Haman to proceed to honor the Jew Mordecai in the ways that he has proposed. Haman is now humiliated, returns home, and tells his wife and friends of his disgrace. These advisers,

*Mordecai, Not Haman, Is Honored*

rather than reassure him, predict his downfall at the hands of the Jewish people. As they are abandoning Haman, the king's eunuchs arrive to escort him to Esther's banquet.

### Religious Ethical Mediation Interpretation

The relationship between King Ahasuerus and Haman has always been precarious because both men are egocentric and want to use power to control others. This chapter exposes the way in which the ego of someone who is embedded in the power structure can have disastrous, even deadly, consequences. Because of his loyalty, Haman felt certain that he would destroy his enemy. His arrogance leads to his humiliation and death instead. Faith leaders must be more conscious of the triangulation of leadership in a power structure that breeds competition and contempt.

In the twenty-first century, there is concern about the dangerousness of public leadership:

> Assessing dangerousness requires a different standard from diagnosing so as to formulate a course of treatment. Dangerousness is about the situation, not the individual; it is more about the effects and the degree of impairment than the specific cause of illness; it does not require a full examination but takes into account whatever information is available.[1]

Examining a Trump election rally offers information that can be taken into account when discussing dangerousness and public leadership. This is the case because a rally is "the performance of a particular worldview."[2] The worldview has three elements: (1) America was once great; (2) America's decline is a result of the action of its enemies; and (3) the solution is Trump himself. The relationship between Trump and his followers is one of devotion because they feel that they are under threat. Consequently, Trump's

1. Brandy X. Lee, "Introduction: Our Duty to Warn and to Protect," in *The Dangerous Case of Donald Trump: 37 Psychiatrists and Mental Health Experts Assess a President*, Updated and Expanded with New Essays (New York: Thomas Dunne, 2019), 5.
2. Stephen D. Reicher and S. Alexander Haslam, "Trump's Appeal: What Psychology Tells Us," *Scientific American*, March 1, 2017, https://www.scientificamerican.com/article/trump-rsquo-s-appeal-what-psychology-tells-us/.

leader-followership relationship depends on loyalty. It is not loyalty per se that is problematic. It is when a leader's expectation for loyalty feeds the "shadows of leadership such as coercive or reward power, deceit, and irresponsibility."[3]

In brief, the relationship between leaders and followers is not solely interpersonal; rather, the interpersonal is situational and political. When we remember that the church is a human institution embedded in a particular cultural, social, economic, political context, ministers must preach and pastor to nurture both the spiritual life and the capacity of their congregants to discern how to engage faithfully as citizens. From the perspective of religious ethical mediation, it is a pastoral imperative to help congregants engage in politics beyond partisan polarization.[4]

---

3. Craig E. Johnson, *Meeting the Ethical Challenges of Leadership: Casting Light or Shadows* (Thousand Oaks, CA: Sage, 2001), chap. 1.

4. For elaboration of this point, see Marcia Riggs, "Beyond Partisan Polarization?" response to *Prophets and Patriots: Faith in Democracy Beyond the Political Divide*, by Ruth Braunstein, Syndicate, April 13, 2021, https://syndicate.network/symposia/theology/prophets-and-patriots/.

# Esther 7

## 7:1–6

### *Esther's Petition at Last*

King Ahasuerus asks Esther again impatiently for her petition and makes this promise: "Even to the half of my kingdom, it shall be fulfilled" (v. 2b). Perhaps, to the king's surprise, Queen Esther makes this request: "If I have won your favor, O king, and if it pleases the king, let my life be given me—that is my petition—and the lives of my people—that is my request" (v. 3). She elaborates the reason for her request thus: "For we have been sold, I and my people, to be destroyed, to be killed, and to be annihilated. If we had been sold merely as slaves, men and women, I would have held my peace; but no enemy can compensate for this damage to the king" (v. 4). King Ahasuerus asks Esther to tell him the name and whereabouts of the person who would do such a thing. Esther emphatically exclaims, "A foe and enemy, this wicked Haman!" (v. 6a).

## 7:7–10

### *Haman's Fate*

The king is distraught and leaves the banquet hall. Meanwhile, a fearful Haman remains with Esther and as he pleads with her, he falls onto the couch where she is sitting. Upon reentering the hall, the king sees Haman in a compromising position with Esther, assumes this is an assault upon the queen, and he is further infuriated. Harbona, one of the eunuchs attending the king, speaks up, drawing attention to the gallows that Haman had built to hang Mordecai. The

**116**                                                    ESTHER 7:7–10

king orders that Haman be hung on those gallows. Haman is hanged
and the king's anger subsides.

### *Religious Ethical Mediation Interpretation*

In this chapter, Esther reveals her identity as she asks the king to save
her people. Her initial deception regarding her identity and manipulative strategy to gain the king's favor can now be evaluated. In the
religious ethical mediation graphic there is an overlapping image of
two cultures, a culture of deception and a culture of moral courage. It
is in the space of that overlap where intercultural encounter occurs,
and this is where an individual acts as a religious ethical mediator.

Esther is standing in the space of the overlapping cultures from
the moment that she entered the palace. Dynamics of patriarchal
privilege and power, anti-Semitism, law vs. justice compose the
culture of deception; dynamics of resistance to oppression, decisions amid moral ambiguity, and group solidarity are features of the
culture of moral courage. When Esther risks going before the king,
reveals her Jewish identity, intercedes on behalf her people, and
names Haman as the enemy of the Jewish people, she mediates the
conflictual dynamics of gender, male power, and ethnic difference.
As one author suggests, Esther operates from an "ethics of deception" as a trickster does.[1] An ethics of deception distinguishes truth
and truthfulness. "Truth is a matter of epistemology and addresses
what is known and knowable; truthfulness is an ethical issue and
deals with the use and manipulation of information."[2] Moreover, in
the context of mediation, "Deception, as operationally defined for
use in mediation, is any manipulation or intervention designed or
calculated to encourage a disputing part to reevaluation or recon-
sider his or her position."[3]

Esther as transformative mediator shifts the energies of conflict between Haman and Mordecai, King Ahasuerus and Haman,

---

1. Robert D. Benjamin, "Managing the Natural Energy of Conflict: Mediators, Tricksters,
and the Constructive Uses of Deception," in *Bringing Peace into the Room: How the Personal
Qualities of the Mediator Impact the Process of Conflict Resolution*, ed. Daniel Bowling and David
Hoffman (San Francisco: Jossey Bass, 2003), 125.

2. Ibid., 127.

3. Ibid.

*Haman's Fate*

Haman and the Jewish people using banquets. The banquets provide pretext and context for her manipulation of persons and issues. The intention behind the manipulation is obvious to us as readers of the story. Still, we must continue to ask about this "means justifies the end" ethical thinking. After all, means-end thinking in this story leads to a "win-lose" conclusion. First, Haman loses his life; second, people within the citadel of Susa and Haman's sons are killed. The winners are Mordecai and the Jewish people; or are they? This question will be interrogated when chapters 8–9 are discussed.

When the oppressed struggle for liberation, their oppressors are alarmed when they speak of obtaining liberation "by any means necessary." The assumption is that this statement is a call to violent revolution. During the civil rights movement in the United States, Malcolm X, considered to be the opposite of Martin Luther King Jr., was known for uttering those words. Malcom X made a speech in 1964 at the founding of the Organization of Afro-American Unity in which he provides this meaning of the phrase:

> That's our motto. We want freedom by any means necessary. We want justice by any means necessary. We want equality by any means necessary. We don't feel that in 1964, living in a country that is supposedly based upon freedom, and supposedly the leader of the free world, we don't think that we should have to sit around and wait for some segregationist congressmen and senators and a President from Texas in Washington, D.C., to make up their minds that our people are due now some degree of civil rights. No, we want it now or we don't think anybody should have it.[4]

He goes on to assert that violence as self-defense is justified because the racist system and persons who are agents of that system are immoral:

> Tactics based solely on morality can only succeed when you are dealing with people who are moral or a system that is moral. A man or system which oppresses a man because of

4. "(1964) Malcolm X's Speech at the Founding Rally of the Organization of Afro-American Unity," BlackPast, October 15, 2007, https://www.blackpast.org/african-american-history /speeches-african-american-history/1964-malcolm-x-s-speech-founding-rally-organization -afro-american-unity/.

his color is not moral. It is the duty of every Afro-American person and every Afro-American community throughout this country to protect its people against mass murderers, against bombers, against lynchers, against floggers, against brutalizers and against exploiters.[5]

Although Malcolm X does endorse violence as self-defense, his argument is consistent with a spiral of violence description of the relationship between oppressors and the oppressed. The spiral of violence asserts that injustice embedded in a system begins the spiral of violence. Revolt by the oppressed is the second dimension of the spiral. The third and final dimension of the spiral is the use of repressive means by the oppressors to stop the revolt.

The class and gender stratification that opens the book as well as the ethnocentrism (exemplified by Haman and Mordecai's relationship, but also intrinsic to imperialist domination of the region by the Persians) establishes the violent systemic injustice of the context. Mordecai and Esther represent the oppressed, along with Mordecai's insubordination to Haman and the infiltration of the empire by the selection of Esther as queen) are earmarks of revolt. Repression was the plot contrived by Haman to hang Mordecai and annihilate all Jews. The spiral is disrupted by Esther's intervention with the king. When we look at what transpires in the story until Esther intervenes, it is not surprising that there is a reversal of roles between the oppressor and oppressed in the concluding chapters. The spiral of violence is important because it provides a lens for understanding how the oppressor and oppressed are caught up in a system of injustice that diminishes and destroys them both.

The year 2021 marked the one-hundred-year anniversary of the Tulsa Race Massacre (May 31–June 1, 1921) in Tulsa, Oklahoma.[6] This Massacre demonstrates the deep historical roots of a white oppressor-Black oppressed relationship enabled through the state-sanctioned injustice of racial violence perpetrated against African Americans. In 1921 the African American community of Greenwood was a thriving economic hub referred to as "Black Wall Street."

5. Ibid.
6. "1921 Tulsa Race Massacre," History.com, May 24, 2024, https://www.history.com/topics/1920s/tulsa-race-massacre.

*Haman's Fate*

This community was looted and burned down, and as many as three hundred Black persons were killed by an angry white mob.

The inciting incident was the arrest of Dick Rowland, a Black male teenager who entered an office building elevator and was later arrested; he was accused of sexually assaulting the white female elevator operator. Men of the African American community desired to protect Rowland while in jail, but the police refused their assistance. Meanwhile white citizens of Tulsa (some armed and deputized by city officials) and others from surrounding towns, fueled by the idea that there was an uprising of Black Tulsans, burned down Greenwood. By the time that the National Guard arrived, and the governor declared martial law, the massacre had occurred.[7]

There was every attempt to cover up this event:

> For decades, there were no public ceremonies, memorials for the dead or any efforts to commemorate the events of May 31–June 1, 1921. Instead, there was a deliberate effort to cover them up.
>
> The *Tulsa Tribune* removed the front-page story of May 31 that sparked the chaos from its bound volumes, and scholars later discovered that police and state militia archives about the riot were missing as well. As a result, until recently the Tulsa Race Massacre was rarely mentioned in history books, taught in schools or even talked about.[8]

There have been efforts since 1996 to commemorate the event as well as to make amends formally through a state government sponsored Tulsa Race Massacre Commission and a bill requiring that this story be taught in schools. Also, there is currently a Tulsa Reparations Coalition sponsored by the Racial Justice Center, Inc., and a reparations bill has been introduced to Congress.[9]

As we reread Esther 7 through the challenge of state-sanctioned violence in the nineteenth, twentieth, and twenty-first centuries that disproportionately kills or incarcerates African Americans and

7. Ibid.
8. Ibid.
9. Ibid.; DeNeen L. Brown, "Reparations Bill for Tulsa Race Massacre Survivors Introduced in Congress," May 21, 2021, *The Washington Post*, https://www.washingtonpost.com/history/2021/05/21/tulsa-massacre-reparations-bill/.

other minoritized people of color, we in the churches must consider what it means to be faithful amid necropolitics.[10] Womanist ethicist Angela D. Sims, author of *Lynched: The Power of Memory in a Culture of Terror*, speaking as a theological educator, succinctly states what is needed:

> In this post-9/11 season, I realize that as an administrator and theological faculty member, I do have a responsibility to create space where students can reflect on ways in which they are both compelled to appeal to the moral conscience of the nation and to articulate an ethics of ecclesiology that demonstrates their understanding of the nature, purpose, and function of church and its relationship to Christ and white supremacy.[11]

What is your ethics of ecclesiology in relation to Christ and white supremacy? To use a category from H. Richard Niebuhr's typology of the church in relation to society, does your ethics promote a church that transforms culture? Or, as liberation theologians might ask, is the church a force for liberation from systemic injustice in church and society?

---

10. Namrata Verghese, "What Is Necropolitics? The Political Calculation of Life and Death," *Teen Vogue*, March 10, 2021, https://www.teenvogue.com/story/what-is-necropolitics. Necropolitics is a framework that illuminates how governments assign differential value to human life. The closer you are to dominant power, the more your life is worth." See also Christophe D. Ringer, *Necropolitics: The Religious Crisis of Mass Incarceration in America* (Lahnham, MD: Lexington Books, 2020).

11. Angela D. Sims, "Realities of Teaching in a Neo-Lynching Culture in 21st Century America," *Religious Studies News*, April 28, 2017, https://rsn.aarweb.org/spotlight-on/theo-ed /between-the-times/realities-teaching-neo-lynching-culture-21st-century-america.

# Esther 8

## 8:1–8

### *Revoking Haman's Orders*

Upon the execution of Haman, King Ahasuerus transfers Haman's status and property to Esther, and he gives the signet ring that he had given Haman to Mordecai. Esther then sets Mordecai over the house of Haman. Esther turns next to the matter of Haman's plot against the Jews. She goes to the king, who again extends the golden scepter to her. This time Esther requests that the king issue an order revoking the letters issued by Haman with the orders to annihilate the Jews. Esther asks, "For how can I bear to see the calamity that is coming on my people? Or how can I bear to see the destruction of my kindred?" (v. 6). The king gives permission to write whatever law or decree is needful regarding the fate of the Jews in the king's name and seal it with the king's ring: "for an edict written in the name of the king and sealed with the king's ring cannot be revoked" (v. 8b).

## 8:9–17

### *Decreeing the Great Reversal*

Mordecai writes the letters revoking Haman's death decree and sends the letters out under the king's seal: "By these letters the king allowed the Jews who were in every city to assemble and defend their lives, to destroy, to kill, and to annihilate any armed force of any people or province that might attack them, with their children and women and to plunder their goods" (v. 11). This act of mass killing is to take place on a single day, the thirteenth day in the month of Adar (v. 12). The writ is issued as a decree from the citadel of

Susa; it is published to all peoples in the provinces, "and the Jews were to be ready on that day to take revenge on their enemies" (v. 13). Mordecai emerges now dressed in royal robes ("blue and white, with a golden crown and a mantle of fine linen and purple" [v. 15]). Meanwhile the Jews in Susa and in all the provinces celebrate, effecting a festival and holiday. "Furthermore, many of the peoples of the country professed to be Jews, because the fear of the Jews had fallen upon them" (v. 17).

### *Religious Ethical Mediation Interpretation*

The theme of reversals in the book of Esther is stark in chapter 8. Esther, a Jewish woman, is given Haman's property and status, and she asks the king to rescind Haman's orders to commit genocide of the Jews. Mordecai receives Haman's signet ring and thus his power and status. He writes and with the signet ring seals the letters that grant Jews the right to defend themselves against the armed force of any people, to kill and destroy the armed forces as well as the women and children, and to plunder their goods. Does this not seem like excessive violence? Have the oppressed truly become the oppressor? And, in verse 17b, other people desire to pass as Jewish: "Furthermore, many of the peoples of the country professed to be Jews, because the fear of the Jews had fallen upon them." Who's passing now?

What kind of violence is Mordecai sanctioning—even for one day? The violence being sanctioned in this chapter can be assessed as preemptive violence or revenge or retaliatory violence. Preemptive violence has a legal basis in international law as a form of self-defense if an attack is imminent. In the twenty-first century the continuing growth of weapons of mass destruction as well as weapons such as drones should make us leery of the effectiveness of preemptive violence. As religious ethical mediators, we must stand in the overlapping space of intercultural encounter and pursue ways to transform conflicts constructively.

Retaliatory violence or revenge is a direct response to violence that has already been inflicted. According to some psychological

*Decreeing the Great Reversal*

scientists, there is a "complicated psychology of revenge."[1] Revenge creates a cycle of retaliation between those seeking revenge and those who are punished; rather than an emotional catharsis, revenge may become a means to "deliver a message." Still, the overriding aim of revenge is to reestablish justice from the point of view of the person or group seeking revenge. But, because there are variable definitions of justice, revenge functions in three ways: (1) deterrence, (2) establishment of acceptable conduct, and (3) "altruistic punishment" (threat of revenge when cooperation fails). These same researchers suggest that more often than revenge the "scale tips in favor of forgiveness." Forgiveness is understood as a "secondary instinct" that has evolved within humans "to suppress the desire for revenge and signal their willingness to continue on, even though someone has harmed their interest, assuming the person will refrain from doing so again in the future."[2]

I am not sure that we have developed forgiveness as a secondary instinct, even for us Christians. Although our overarching model for forgiveness is a forgiving God (Luke 23:34), and we have numerous teachings attributed to Jesus about forgiveness (e.g., Matt. 18:21–22; Luke 6:37), we Christians do not tend to forgive unconditionally, and our theologies of collective forgiveness are most often politicized. For example, we grant ourselves divine authority to determine who is worthy of forgiveness, especially in the face of mass tragedy, such as September 11, 2001. In the poem titled, "9/11/01–9/17/01,"[3] African American poet Lucille Clifton points out how Americans thought that we were undeserving of the "villainy" that the 9/11 attack represented. Clifton reminds us that forgiveness requires us to be self-reflective about who we are and how we are participants (covertly or overtly) in wrongs that are the basis of mass tragedy. We must scrutinize our liturgies of forgiveness to ensure that our confessions do not reinscribe notions of moral superiority. We must confess our complicity in creating the conditions for our own violent undoing.

1. Eric Jaffe, "The Complicated Psychology of Revenge," *Observer*, October 4, 2011, https://www.psychologicalscience.org/observer/the-complicated-psychology-of-revenge.
2. Ibid.
3. Lucille Clifton, "9/11/01-9/17/01," in *September 11, 2001: American Writers Respond*, ed. William Heyen (Silver Spring, MD: Etruscan Press, 2002), 80–84.

Finally, considering what happens in Esther 8, these questions propel us into Esther 9: Who is the oppressed, and who is the oppressor now? Has not the threat, Haman, been removed? Why not seek less violent means to ensure the safety and welfare of the Jewish people?

# Esther 9

## 9:1–10

### *The Mass Killing of the Enemies of the Jewish People*

On the thirteenth day of the month of Adar, the killing of the enemies of the Jewish people throughout the provinces of King Ahasuerus commences. The people and the officials of the provinces fear Mordecai. "So the Jews struck down all their enemies with the sword, slaughtering, and destroying them, and did as they pleased to those who hated them" (v. 5).

Although they killed the ten sons of Haman, they "did not touch the plunder" (v. 10).

## 9:11–15

### *Queen Esther Makes an Additional Request of the King*

The king informs Queen Esther that five hundred people in the citadel of Susa and the sons of Haman have been killed by the Jews and asks if she has another request, assuring her that he will grant her petition. She requests that the Jews in Susa be granted an extra day to kill their enemies and to hang the sons of Haman. The king commanded that the queen's request be fulfilled. Since they are already dead, Haman's sons are hung in public as an act of shaming. On the fourteenth day of Adar, the Jews of Susa killed three hundred persons, but again they did not touch the plunder.

## Religious Ethical Mediation Interpretation

This chapter is particularly difficult to read. The interpretive lens of the omnipresence of violence becomes manifest through the extreme reversal of power that enables Mordecai to decree mass murder of those who are named enemies of the Jews. Likewise, Esther moves from her position as religious ethical mediator who stands in the overlapping space between a culture of deception and a culture of moral courage. She is now firmly complicit with Mordecai in his power play to gain a place in the monarchy. In fact, she is responsible for the hanging of Haman's dead sons and the public shaming that ensues. She has relinquished her role as a transformative mediator. This is then an ethical lesson of this chapter: Moral agency as a religious ethical mediator requires vigilance on the part of anyone who seeks to live as one. Esther lost sight of the transformative role that she had been playing.

In the present post-9/11 context of Islamophobia and ongoing Middle East struggle between the Palestinian and Jewish peoples, a question emerges about how to understand the killing committed by the Jews in this chapter. The question is, however, not about *who* does the killing; I am concerned with *how* and *why* mass killing happens by whomever.

The text informs us that the killing is lawful. King Ahasuerus authorizes Mordecai to write letters that permit the Jews in all the provinces to gather to defend themselves and the letters are sealed with his ring, thus this edict will in effect override the previous one to kill the Jews issued by Haman. Although the letters permit the Jews to defend themselves, the killing ordered by Haman had not actually begun; so is the killing by the Jews preemptive violence rather than self-defense? Is it an act of aggression? In either case, is it justifiable? The arguments in support of such violence are most often related to legal justification (which the edict grants), but there are other conditions such as imminent threat that may serve as justification.

Although I do not want our ethical reflection here to become mired in philosophical theories about justifications for violence and war, I do want us to reflect about religiously motivated violence in

*Queen Esther Makes an Additional Request of the King*

the twentieth and twenty-first centuries.[1] We tend to think of Islam and other religions as violent, but Christianity has sanctioned violence to advance the spread of Christianity as well as the basis of religiously motivated violence as in the bombing of abortion clinics.[2] Religiously motivated violence is grounded in ideas about us vs. them, cosmic war, and martyrs vs. demons. In brief,

> We are acutely aware that throughout history when human conflicts have been validated by religious sanction they are intensified. God has been claimed to be on both sides of every war. This has been possible because each of the great world faiths has either assumed or asserted its own unique superiority as the one and only true faith and path to the highest good—in familiar Christian terms, to salvation. These exclusive claims to absolute truth have exacerbated the division of the human community into rival groups, and have repeatedly been invoked in support of oppression, slavery, conquest, and exploitation.[3]

Moreover, using the religious ethical mediation interpretive lens, this chapter pushes us to consider the relationship between law and ethics and how such may function as part of a culture of deception. In this chapter, there are clearly legal grounds for the actions that take place. In this text, it is not the distinction between law and ethics that concerns us. It is the collapse of the legal grounds for the killing of the enemies of the Jews into an ethical justification that is troubling. This happens in Esther because of this perspective: "Israelite law is divine in origin and linked to God's sense of justice and holiness (Exod. 20; Lev. 19:1–2)."[4] However, "laws [in Esther] are the vehicles through which the characters accomplish their goals and laws are obstacles which provide suspense and challenge through

---

1. Charlotte Brandon, "Is Pre-emptive War Ever Justified?" E-*International Relations*, June 8, 2011, https://www.e-ir.info/2011/06/08/is-pre-emptive-war-ever-justified/; "Just War Theory," *Internet Encyclopedia of Philosophy*, https://iep.utm.edu/justwar/.
2. See Kenneth R. Chase and Alan Jacobs, *Must Christianity Be Violent? Reflections on History, Practice, and Theology* (Grand Rapids: Brazos, 2003), and Mark Jurgensmeyer, *Terror in the Mind of God: The Global Rise of Religious Violence* (Berkeley: University of California Press, 2000), chap. 2.
3. Jurgensmeyer, *Terror in the Mind of God*, x.
4. Elsie R. Stern, "Esther and the Politics of Diaspora," *Jewish Quarterly Review* (Winter 2010): 33.

the narrative," and law in Esther is consistent with the themes of excess and reversal.[5]

The excess of law is evident in trivial matters (how much to drink, 1:8), to rituals (how to prepare virgins for the harem, 8:12), to appearances before the king (how to handle uninvited appearances, 4:11, 16) and "the gravest of matters—extermination of the Jews (3:12–13; 4:8), and the extermination of their enemies (8:13–14; 9:1, 14–15)."[6] Law is identified with the will of the king, not identified with the will of God. Likewise, despite the claim that an edict of the king cannot be revoked, the reversal of the edict to kill the Jews is revoked and replaced by another. In summary,

> Esther's portrait of law meticulously reverses the central biblical myths regarding law in the land of Israel. In Esther's Shushan, there is an overabundance of law which is intimately linked to the will of the king, rather than to the will of God. Despite its patently subjective and capricious origins, it can become eternal and irrevocable. Despite the ritualized canonization and irreversibility of law, there are often no legal consequences for transgressions.[7]

Using the religious ethical interpretive lens again, we are pushed to consider that the collapse of a relationship between law and ethics is a dynamic of a culture of deception. In this chapter, there are clearly legal grounds for the actions that take place, and we see that which is legal is not always ethical. Even when we can offer a legal justification for killing, this ethical question remains: What are the motivations of those who commit the killing? Although it can be difficult to determine the motivations of others, we can engage in self-examination of our motives considering larger goals, purposes, or ends that we seek. On one hand, the goal of the mass killing is to protect the Jewish community. On the other hand, the goal might be to instill fear to control those who are considered "enemies." From the perspective of religious ethical mediation, both motivations could be refocused by a goal of living together respectfully because both

5. Ibid., 35.
6. Ibid.
7. Ibid., 36.

*Inauguration of the Feast of Purim*                                          **129**

groups imagine themselves interconnected in a web that includes their enemies.

# 9:16–32

## *Inauguration of the Feast of Purim*

The Jews in the king's provinces killed seventy-five thousand of their enemies on the thirteenth day of Adar, "and on the fourteenth day, they rested and made that a day of feasting and gladness" (v. 17b). The Jews in Susa gathered on the thirteenth and fourteenth day, and they made the fifteenth day their day of feasting. The final use of the law is the establishment of Purim (9:20–32). Queen Esther, along with Mordecai, writes two letters; one records what happened and the other ordered the days and practices of Purim.

The fourteenth day of Adar is honored as a day of feasting and gladness by the Jews of the villages, "a holiday on which they send gifts of food to one another." (v. 19c) Mordecai sends letters to all the Jews in the provinces instructing them to celebrate on the fourteenth and fifteenth of Adar annually, "as the days on which the Jews gained relief from their enemies, and as the month that had been turned for them from sorrow into gladness and from mourning into a holiday; that they should make these days of feasting and gladness, days for sending gifts of food to one another and presents to the poor. So the Jews adopted as a custom what they had begun to do, as Mordecai had written to them" (vv. 22–23). The day of celebration is named Purim because Haman had cast Pur—the lot—in deciding to destroy the Jews. (v. 24) Purim was authorized by Queen Esther along with Mordecai and confirmed by written letter: "Letters were sent wishing peace and security to all the Jews, to the one hundred twenty-seven provinces of the kingdom of Ahasuerus, and giving orders that these days of Purim should be observed at their appointed seasons, as the Jew Mordecai and Queen Esther enjoined on the Jews, just as they laid down for themselves and for the descendants regulations concerning their fasts and lamentations. The command of Esther fixed these practices of Purim, and it was recorded in writing" (vv. 30–32).

### Religious Ethical Mediation Interpretation

#### A Lesson from Purim

An article titled "The Esther Narratives as Reminders—for Jews and for Christians" offers reasons from the narrative why the Purim tradition is important. First,

> it illustrates how the distress, menace and despair of individuals and a whole community can be changed to salvation, joy and the courage to live. Second, the book shows how important it is to take one's own initiative and to combine such initiative with cooperation—things do not just change by themselves. Third, at the same time, the story points to the fact that not everything is within human power: the rescue only succeeds through the interaction of human involvement and fateful turns of events. Fourth, the text optimistically promotes trust in the existence of order and of an authority in charge of it.[8]

When we read the book of Esther as parody and comedy that uses hyperbole to depict the behaviors and characters of the Persian rulers, then the book of Esther presents another perspective on how diasporic Jews outwit their oppressors and survive. The Esther narrative is about Jewish survival, but it is unlike the Exodus narrative of Jewish liberation and the covenantal paradigm of the Jewish relationship to God. "In Esther history is ruled by accident; there is no stabilizing paradigm. So even though the story ends happily for the Jews, the narrative offers no guarantee that this course of events will repeat itself next time."[9] Still, Esther is read publicly during the festival of Purim, thus its importance to Jewish tradition and identity is significant.

We Christians must grapple with the ending of this book because it is part of our canon. The killing that makes possible the

---

8. Veronika Bachmann, "The Esther Narratives as Reminders—for Jews and for Christians," *European Judaism* 47, no.1 (Spring 2014): 119. According to the *Holocaust Encyclopedia*: "Purim is a Jewish holiday marking the deliverance of the Jews from a royal death decree. According to the Jewish lunar calendar, Purim usually falls during February or March. *Purim*, the Hebrew word meaning *lots*, named for the lots that Ham cast in order to determine the day on which he would kill the Jews. The mood of the holiday is lively and playful, celebrating the near escape from death, https://encyclopedia.ushmm.org/content/en/article/purim.

9. Stern, "Esther and the Politics of Diaspora," 45.

*Inauguration of the Feast of Purim*

Jewish victory pushes us to consider how both the oppressed and the oppressor perpetuate violence and experience loss. Losses may be physical (lives, property), but there are spiritual and psychological losses also. Both groups are forever haunted by grief and trauma that is not short-lived. In the aftermath of mass tragedy or living for years in conditions of intractable conflict, the impact is intergenerational trauma for individuals and the community.

Importantly, womanist practical theologian Phillis Sheppard writes about trauma "as a force, not as an event, operative between the individual and the social and public milieu, on the psyche and in group processes, and permeating the social structures that shape public and private life."[10] We must examine how the church as a social institution is or is not fulfilling its role in healing collective grief and trauma. It is important that we in the churches respect the street memorials after mass tragedies as sacred spaces where healing is taking place. How shall the church extend its ministry into these sacred spaces and provide public spiritual direction?

---

10. Phillis Sheppard, "Social Trauma and Public Spirituality: A Womanist Relational Ethic of Spiritual Practice," in *Kaleidoscope: Broadening the Palette in the Art of Spiritual Direction*, ed. Ineda P. Adesanya (New York: Church Publishing, 2019), 137.

# Esther 10

## 10:1–3

### *A Postscript*

The book ends where it began: asserting the monarchial and patriarchal power of King Ahasuerus and now Mordecai. Two men are in power. The king has prospered, and he has promoted Mordecai to royal status. "For Mordecai the Jew was next in rank to King Ahasuerus, and he was powerful among the Jews and popular with his many kindred, for he sought the good of his people and interceded for the welfare of all his descendants" (v. 3).

### *Religious Ethical Mediation Interpretation*

It is interesting that a book named for a woman, Esther, ends exalting a man, Mordecai. Perhaps we can simply attribute this to the political, social, and cultural reality of the time. However, it is too often the reality in our churches. Senior leadership positions are filled by men who may not be as qualified as women. It took the joint efforts of Esther and Mordecai to ensure the survival of their community. When will we acknowledge collaborative leadership, particularly partnerships between women and men, as normative for how to live out being created in the image of God (Gen. 1:27)? Overall, the book of Esther should push us to think about how morally ambiguous our choices often are. We Christians have many stories of religiously motivated violence in the past and in the present. Our challenge is to be faithful to a larger vision of God's justice; we live in the omnipresence of violence and must pray that our choices align with that vision.

# *Postscript*

When I was given the opportunity to write a theological commentary on Ruth and Esther, I was excited. In the Black church where I grew up and was ordained, these two books were favorites as stories about courageous outsider women. Ruth and Esther have been and continue as role models for African American women and are the texts for preachers for many Women's Day services in the church. Moreover, Ruth's vow of loyalty (act of *hesed*) and Esther's profession of sacrifice for her community (an act of moral courage) earmarked their strength under conditions of marginality and threat. Surely these women's stories offer the perfect biblical role models for Black women (and men) who must live into the interconnections between our individual and communal survival. This was my point of departure.

However, my focus and ability to write this commentary came under attack, and a year-long project became a six-year struggle. I suffered the personal losses of African American women close to me, including the death of my mother. Likewise, there was the mounting number of deaths of African American women as the result of state violence. All of this made it more crucial that I read these books as commentary on gendered violence.

As I read womanist and other women of color biblical scholars' interpretations of Ruth and Esther, I became convicted that applying my religious ethical mediation hermeneutic to these texts might provide insights for us about living faithfully amid gendered violence. Reading with womanists, feminists, and postcolonial scholars instructed, emboldened, and overwhelmed me because at times their interpretations of the texts exposed biased translations and readings of the text with which I had not yet grappled and will need to continue to grapple. Their scholarship pushed me to consider the texts in ways that I had never imagined. I do hope that I have understood and engaged their scholarship respectfully.

Likewise, I hope that these biblical scholars can accept my hermeneutic as a valid way to open the text ethically and theologically for readers like me who are not experts in biblical exegesis and hermeneutics. My religious ethical mediation hermeneutic is my way of reading the text as an ethicist. As I read the text, ethical questions and historical and current events came to mind. My interpretation represents what I see happening in the text in dialogue with what has happened and is happening in our social context. My religious ethical mediation interpretative framework leads me to expose how interpersonal, intercultural, and intercommunal encounters are rooted in intersectional gendered violence and how Ruth or Esther responds or does not respond to such as a religious ethical mediator. My interpretations offer ethical questions and challenges that are not traditional theological reflection found in a commentary.

Also, writing amid the #BlackLivesMatter and #SayHerName movements has pushed me to think about what it means to write a theological commentary as a womanist ethicist. I do ethics to help persons of faith and Christian communities of faith understand that we can be intentional and unintentional perpetrators of the violence that routinely silences or kills African American women and girls and all Others who are a threat to the power and privileges of white supremacy and heteropatriarchy. As was the case historically, Christians have designated some groups of people to be either without souls or deemed irredeemable. Christianity has been a weapon to enslave and continues to be used to control groups of people.

My interpretative lens is that of a womanist ethicist who regards violence as constitutive of our social context and central to conflicts that drive our interrelationships as social groups. I use the term "the omnipresence of violence" to describe this reality. I use this term to remind us that violence is pervasive rather than episodic, and there are many forms of violence in which we participate and/or to which we fall victim: for example, cultural, psychological, spiritual,

# POSTSCRIPT

economic, and political violence, without being fully aware of the harm being committed by or upon us. Indeed, I think that we should push ourselves to consider how we live complicitly with the omnipresence of violence. It is complicity that harms both others and ourselves because this is how we deceive ourselves into bibliolatry (worship of the Bible), literalism (worship of the text), or culturalism (conforming the Bible to the norms of the culture).[1] Having written this commentary, I am certain that how I preach the books of Ruth and Esther going forward will differ from any of my previous sermons. I hope that this will be the case for others as well.

No one needs to speculate about the omnipresence of violence in our society today. Currently in the United States mass shootings and murders happen regularly and in varied contexts—schools, churches, nightclubs, theaters, parades. The public debate about gun violence seems to have two primary foci. First, there are advocates who argue for the protection of the right of citizens to own guns. Supporters of this right tend to argue from an interpretation of the Second Amendment, which they say is based upon the original intent of the nation's founders. Second, others are concerned about gun control, the control of gun violence by means such as raising the age limit for the purchase of guns, banning assault-style weapons, and compiling a national database on gun sales. In this context of mass killings and polarized public policy debate about guns, the churches and other faith communities have the difficult tasks of mourning the dead, healing families and communities, as well as educating communities and individuals about gun violence and control.

Consequently, we are called to nurture a consciousness and way of being in the world centered in nonviolent resistance. Nonviolent resistance is a commitment to transform the violence of "imperialist white supremacist capitalist patriarchy."[2] We must grapple to find ethical responses amid social, cultural, political, and economic pressures that bear down upon us. Religious ethical mediators are committed to nonviolent resistance as transformative mediators of conflict.

---

1. Peter Gomes, *The Good Book*, as cited in Yvette A. Flunder, *Where the Edge Gathers: Building a Community of Radical Inclusion* (Cleveland: Pilgrim, 2005), 23.
2. bell hooks, *Writing Beyond Race* (New York: Routledge, 2013), 16.

Religious ethical mediation as an interpretative framework pushes us to recognize that the conflict that derives from differences of interpretation of texts, events, and one another cannot be ignored. Interpretation is not passive; it requires us to interrogate the subject or object of interpretation as well as ourselves. Interrogation leads either to further inquiry or to intractable conflict. Further inquiry suggests the possibility of dialogue; without that dialogical possibility, intractable conflict ensues because we make assumptions rather than ask questions for clarity or empathize to understand. Conflict is part of the dialogical possibility when we recognize its generative quality. Generative conflict means that we are open to unexpected responses as well as to not finding answers, at least not immediately. Interpretation is active as we allow for generative conflict with texts, events, and one another.

This reading of the books of Ruth and Esther has been active interpretation. I found myself in conflict with the texts as I lost my naiveté about Ruth and Esther as women who had been role models for so long. They are not exemplars of commitment or sacrifice. They are women who struggled to be moral agents of their destinies, and that is a healthier interpretation for Black women, and all women. I found myself in tension sometimes with biblical scholars whose interpretations seemed primarily deconstructive. Still, I am grateful for their interpretations because they pushed me to grapple with how to write my authentic interpretation of the texts based upon my religious ethical mediation hermeneutic. Likewise, I invite you to turn to this commentary for insights—not answers—that may inform your interpretation of these two books.

Finally, I am a womanist ethicist who has written a commentary that I suspect will not be received by some readers as a theological commentary. However, it is a theological commentary consistent with my belief that theology and ethics for the twenty-first-century church must derive from reading the Bible as commentary on social justice issues in history and in our time. We must read biblical texts and ask questions along with other faithful Christians about how to be moral agents who seek to diminish our complicity in the omnipresence of violence.

# Selected Bibliography

Akoto, Dorothy Bea. "Esther." In *The Africana Bible: Reading Israel's Scriptures from Africa and the Africana Diaspora*, Hugh R. Page, general editor, 268–72 . Minneapolis: Fortress, 2010.

Anderson, Cheryl B. *Ancient Laws and Contemporary Controversies: The Need for Inclusive Biblical Interpretation*. New York: Oxford University Press, 2009.

Bailey, Randall, Benny Liew Tat-siong, and Fernando F. Segovia, eds. *They Were All Together in One Place? Toward Minority Biblical Criticism*. Atlanta: Society of Biblical Literature, 2009.

Bechtel, Carol M. *Esther*. Interpretation: A Bible Commentary for Teaching and Preaching. Louisville, KY: John Knox, 2002.

Brock, Rita Nakashima, et al. *Off the Menu: Asian and Asian North American Women's Religion and Theology*. Louisville, KY: Westminster John Knox Press, 2007.

Byron, Gay L., and Vanessa Lovelace, eds. *Womanist Interpretations of the Bible: Expanding the Discourse*. Atlanta: SBL Press, 2016.

Cannon, Katie G. *Katie's Cannon: Womanism and the Soul of the Black Community*. New York: Continuum, 1995.

Cottrill, Amy C. *Reading Biblical Narratives as an Ethical Project*. Louisville, KY: Westminster John Knox Press, 2021.

Day, Linda, and Carolyn Pressler. *Engaging the Bible in a Gendered World*. Louisville, KY: Westminster John Knox Press, 2006.

Donaldson, Laura F. and Kwok Pui-lan, eds. *Postcolonialism, Feminism, and Religious Discourse*. New York: Routledge, 2002.

Dube, Musa W. *Postcolonial Feminist Interpretation of the Bible*. Saint Louis: Chalice, 2000.

———, ed. *Other Ways of Reading: African Women and the Bible*. Atlanta: Society of Biblical Literature, 2002.

Dunbar, Ericka Shawndricka. *Trafficking Hadassah: Collective Trauma, Cultural Memory, and Identity in the Book of Esther and in the African Diaspora*. New York: Routledge, 2022.

Gafney, Wilda. "Ruth." In *The Africana Bible: Reading Israel's Scriptures from Africa and the Africana Diaspora*, Hugh R. Page, general editor, 249–54. Minneapolis: Fortress, 2010.

———. *Womanist Midrash: A Reintroduction to Women of the Torah and the Throne*. Louisville, KY: Westminster John Knox Press, 2017.

Junior, Nyasha. *An Introduction to Womanist Biblical Interpretation*. Louisville, KY: Westminster John Knox Press, 2015.

Kwok, Pui-lan. *Postcolonial Imagination and Feminist Theology*. Louisville, KY: Westminster John Knox Press, 2005.

Masenya, Madipoane (Ngwan'a Mphahlele), "Esther and Northern Sotho Stories: An African-South African Woman's Commentary." In *Other Ways of Reading: African Women and The Bible*. Edited by Musa W. Dube. Atlanta: Society of Biblical Literature, 2001.

———. "Ruth." In *Global Bible Commentary*, Daniel Patte, general editor, 86–91. Nashville: Abingdon, 2004.

McTernan, Oliver, *Violence in God's Name: Religion in an Age of Conflict*. Maryknoll, NY: Orbis Books, 2003.

Media Education Foundation. "10 Things Men Can Do to Prevent Gender Violence." https://mediaed.org/handouts/10 -Things-Men-Can-Do.pdf.

Newsom, Carol A., and Sharon H. Ringe, eds. *Women's Bible Commentary*. Expanded Edition. Louisville, KY: Westminster John Knox Press, 1998.

Niditch, Susan. "Esther: Folklore, Wisdom, Feminism and Authority" in *A Feminist Companion to Esther, Judith, and Susanna*. Sheffield: Sheffield Academic, 1995, 26–46.

Peters, Rebecca Todd. *Trust Women: A Progressive Christian Argument for Reproductive Justice*. Boston: Beacon, 2018.

SELECTED BIBLIOGRAPHY                                    **139**

Sakenfeld, Katharine Doob. *Just Wives?: Stories of Power and Survival in the Old Testament and Today.* Louisville, KY: Westminster John Knox Press, 2003.

Schüssler Fiorenza, Elisabeth. *Wisdom Ways: Introducing Feminist Biblical Interpretation.* Maryknoll, NY: Orbis Books, 2001.

"Silence Is Not Spiritual" Statement. http://www.silenceisnotspiritual .org/statement.

Smith, Mitzi J., ed. *I Found God in Me: A Womanist Biblical Hermeneutics.* Eugene, OR: Cascade, 2015.

———. "Womanism, Intersectionality, and Biblical Justice." *Mutuality* (Summer 2016). https://www.cbeinternational .org/resources/article/mutuality/womanism-intersectionality -and-biblical-justice.

———. *Womanist Sass and Talk-Back: Social (In)Justice, Intersectionality, and Biblical Interpretation.* Eugene, OR: Cascade, 2018.

Sugirtharajah, R. S. *Exploring Postcolonial Biblical Criticism: History, Method, and Practice.* Wiley, Blackwell, 2012.

Tull, Patricia K. *Esther and Ruth.* Louisville, KY: Westminster John Knox Press, 2003.

Walker, Alice. *In Search of Our Mothers' Gardens: Womanist Prose.* San Diego: Harcourt Brace Jovanovich, 1983.

Weems, Renita J. "Reading Her Way Through the Struggle: African American Women and the Bible." In *Stony the Road We Trod: African American Biblical Interpretation,* edited by Cain Hope Felder, 57–77. Minneapolis: Fortress, 1991.

———. *Battered Love: Marriage, Sex, and Violence in the Hebrew Prophets.* Minneapolis: Fortress, 1995.

———. "Re-Reading for Liberation: African American Women and the Bible." In *Womanist Theological Ethics: A Reader,* edited by Katie Geneva Cannon, Emilie M. Townes, and Angela D. Sims, 51–63 . Louisville, KY: Westminster John Knox Press, 2011.

Wijk-Bos, Johanna W. H. *Ruth and Esther: Women in Alien Lands.* Nashville: Abingdon, 2001.

Williams, Delores S. *Sisters in the Wilderness: The Challenge of Womanist God-Talk.* Maryknoll, NY: Orbis Books, 1993.

Wong Wai Ching Angela. "Esther." In *Global Bible Commentary*, Daniel Patte, general editor, 135–40. Nashville: Abingdon, 2004.

# Index of Scripture

## Old Testament

**Genesis**
| | |
|---|---|
| 1:27 | 132 |
| 12:10 | 27 |
| 19:30–38 | 26, 48 |
| 21:1 | 64 |
| 24:28 | 22n6 |
| 38 | 62 |

**Exodus** **130**
| | |
|---|---|
| 20 | 127 |

**Leviticus**
| | |
|---|---|
| 18 | 62 |
| 19 | 28 |
| 19:1–2 | 127 |
| 19:9–10 | 28, 48 |
| 20 | 62 |
| 23 | 28 |

**Numbers**
| | |
|---|---|
| 22–24 | 26, 48 |
| 25 | 41–42 |
| 25:1–5 | 26 |

**Deuteronomy** 107
| | |
|---|---|
| 10–14 | 3 |
| 23:3–6 | 26 |
| 23:5 | 48 |
| 23:21–23 | 42 |
| 23:22 | 48 |
| 24 | 28 |
| 24:19 | 28 |
| 24:19–22 | 48 |
| 25 | 42 |

| | |
|---|---|
| 25:1–10 | 62 |
| 25:5 | 61 |
| 25:5–10 | 28, 61 |
| 25:6 | 61 |
| 25:9 | 61–62 |
| 28:23–24 | 27 |
| 28:38–42 | 27 |

**Judges** 21, 32, 64
| | |
|---|---|
| 3:12–30 | 26 |
| 4:17–22 | 3 |
| 16:4–22 | 3 |
| 19 | 3 |

**Ruth** 21–67
| | |
|---|---|
| 1 | 21–45, 67 |
| 1:1–4 | 38 |
| 1:1–5 | 26–33 |
| 1:6 | 63 |
| 1:6–18 | 33–40 |
| 1:6b | 33 |
| 1:8 | 33 |
| 1:8a | 22 |
| 1:16 | 33 |
| 1:16–18 | 39 |
| 1:19–22 | 40–45 |
| 1:20 | 42 |
| 1:20b | 22 |
| 1:21 | 42 |
| 2 | 46–50, 67 |
| 2:1–3 | 46 |
| 2:2a | 46 |
| 2:4–17 | 46 |
| 2:5 | 44, 46 |
| 2:6 | 44 |
| 2:9 | 46, 48 |

| | |
|---|---|
| 2:10 | 46 |
| 2:11 | 48 |
| 2:12 | 46 |
| 2:13 | 46 |
| 2:16 | 47 |
| 2:18–23 | 47–50 |
| 2:20 | 47 |
| 2:22 | 48 |
| 3 | 51–58, 67 |
| 3:1 | 51, 52 |
| 3:1–5 | 51 |
| 3:4 | 51 |
| 3:6–9 | 51 |
| 3:6–15 | 51–52 |
| 3:9 | 44, 53–54 |
| 3:9a | 44 |
| 3:10–11 | 51 |
| 3:10–15a | 54 |
| 3:11 | 28, 43 |
| 3:12–15 | 52 |
| 3:16 | 44 |
| 3:16–18 | 52–58 |
| 4 | 59–67 |
| 4:1–2 | 59 |
| 4:3–6 | 59, 62–63 |
| 4:5 | 61 |
| 4:6 | 61 |
| 4:7–10 | 59 |
| 4:9 | 62 |
| 4:9–10 | 59 |
| 4:10 | 66 |
| 4:11–12 | 60–63 |
| 4:13 | 63 |
| 4:13–17 | 63–64 |
| 4:15a | 63 |
| 4:15b | 63 |

# INDEX OF SCRIPTURE

**Ruth** (*continued*)
| | |
|---|---|
| 4:16 | 66 |
| 4:17 | 63, 66 |
| 4:18–22 | 64–67 |

**1 Samuel**
| | |
|---|---|
| 1:6–7 | 3 |
| 1:8 | 64 |
| 15 | 97 |

**2 Samuel**
| | |
|---|---|
| 7:27 | 60 |
| 13:11–14 | 3 |
| 21 | 27 |

**Ezra** 21, 72
| | |
|---|---|
| 9–10 | 28 |

**Nehemiah** 21, 72

**Judith** 27

**Esther** 71–132
| | |
|---|---|
| 1 | 75–85, 93, 107 |
| 1:1–9 | 75 |
| 1:8 | 128 |
| 1:10–22 | 76–85 |
| 1:19–20 | 101 |
| 1:20–22 | 83, 98 |
| 2 | 86–95, 107 |
| 2:1–4 | 86 |
| 2:5–11 | 86 |
| 2:7 | 72 |
| 2:12–14 | 107–8 |
| 2:12–18 | 87–92 |
| 2:17 | 87 |
| 2:18b | 87 |
| 2:19–23 | 92–95 |
| 2:21–22 | 93 |
| 3 | 96–99, 107 |
| 3:1–6 | 96 |
| 3:6b | 96 |
| 3:7–11 | 96 |
| 3:8 | 97 |
| 3:10–11 | 96 |
| 3:12–13 | 128 |
| 3:12–15 | 97–99 |
| 3:13 | 97 |
| 3:15b | 97 |
| 4 | 100–103, 107, 108–9 |
| 4:1–3 | 100 |
| 4:1b | 100 |
| 4:3b | 100 |
| 4:4–8 | 100 |
| 4:7 | 100 |
| 4:8 | 100, 128 |
| 4:9–17 | 100–103 |
| 4:11 | 109, 128 |
| 4:13–14 | 109 |
| 4:13–15 | 101 |
| 4:14b | 102 |
| 4:16 | 109, 128 |
| 4:16b | 101 |
| 5 | 104–11 |
| 5–7 | 109 |
| 5:1–8 | 104 |
| 5:9–14 | 104–11 |
| 5:11 | 104 |
| 6 | 112–14 |
| 6:1–5 | 112 |
| 6:6–9 | 112 |
| 6:9c | 112 |
| 6:10–14 | 112–14 |
| 7 | 115–20 |
| 7:1–6 | 115 |
| 7:2b | 115 |
| 7:3 | 115 |
| 7:3–10 | 102 |
| 7:4 | 115 |
| 7:6a | 115 |
| 7:7–10 | 115–20 |
| 8 | 121–24 |
| 8–9 | 117 |
| 8:1–8 | 121 |
| 8:6 | 121 |
| 8:8b | 121 |
| 8:9–17 | 121–24 |
| 8:11 | 121 |
| 8:12 | 121, 128 |
| 8:13 | 122 |
| 8:13–14 | 128 |
| 8:15 | 122 |
| 8:17 | 122 |
| 8:17b | 122 |
| 9 | 124–31 |
| 9:1 | 128 |
| 9:1–10 | 125 |
| 9:11–15 | 125–28 |
| 9:14–15 | 128 |
| 9:17b | 129 |
| 9:19c | 129 |
| 9:20–32 | 129 |
| 9:22–23 | 129 |
| 9:24 | 129 |
| 9:30–32 | 129 |
| 10 | 132 |
| 10:1–3 | 132 |
| 10:3 | 132 |

**Job** 43
| | |
|---|---|
| 33:30 | 63 |

**Psalms**
| | |
|---|---|
| 19:7 | 63 |
| 23:3 | 63–64 |

**Proverbs**
| | |
|---|---|
| 12:4 | 43 |
| 31:10 | 28, 43 |

**Ecclesiastes** 71

**Song of Songs** 71n1
| | |
|---|---|
| 3:4 | 22n6 |
| 8:2 | 22n6 |

**Lamentations** 71n1
| | |
|---|---|
| 1:11 | 63 |
| 1:16 | 63 |
| 1:19 | 63 |

**Daniel** 72

**Hosea**
| | |
|---|---|
| 1–3 | 3 |

## *New Testament*

**Matthew**
| | |
|---|---|
| 18:21–22 | 123 |

**Luke**
| | |
|---|---|
| 6:37 | 123 |

# Index of Subjects

*Page numbers in italic refer to figures.*

abduction of women, 3, 38, 90
ableism, 94
abortion, 83–85, 127
Abraham, 27
abuse, eight ways to challenge, 82–83
action/actions
    of God, 32, 63
    human, 71, 74
Adar, month of, 97, 121, 125, 129
Africa, 29
    and "trickster" tradition, 54–56, 108, 116
    *See also individual names/scholars*
African American women, 10–13, 40, 55, 133–34. *See also* Black women; individual names
Agagites, 96–97
agency
    human, 74
    subjective, 107
    *See also* moral agency
agents of justice, 18
Ahasuerus, King, 107
    decrees of (*see* decrees)
    golden scepter of, 101, 104, 121
    half the kingdom offered to Esther by, 104, 115
    and Haman (*see* Haman)
    monarchial and patriarchal power of, 75–76, 94, 132
    Mordecai as saving, 74, 112

    murder plot against, 92–95
    patriarchal power of, 132
    and Queen Vashti's demotion (*see* Vashti, Queen)
    search for new queen/choosing Esther as queen, 74, 86–92, 96
    signet ring of, 96, 121–22
    sleepless night of, 112
    worldview of, 87–88
Akoto, Dorothy Bea (nee Abutiate), 74
Alpert, Rebecca, 35, 38
altruism, 57
"altruistic punishment," 123
ambiguity, moral, 108, 116
Anderson, Cheryl B., 11
Anglican Alliance, 91–92
anti-Semitism, 73, 89, 116
apathy, 111
Asia, 29
Asian Americans, 98–99
Asian, Asian American and Pacific Islander (AAPI) community, 98–99
assimilation, 37, 43, 45, 56, 87–89

Baartman, Sara, 77
Bachmann, Veronika, 130, 130n8
Bailey, Randall C., 97
banquets, 75, 117
    Esther's first and second, 104–5

**143**

**144** INDEX OF SUBJECTS

barley/barley harvest, 5, 28, 40–41, 47,
    51–52
    six measures of barley, 51–52
barrenness, 40, 42
Barth, Karl, xiii
beauty
    of Esther, 86–87
    of Ruth, 48, 56
    standards of, 49–50, 89
    of Vashti, 76
Bellis, Alice Ogden, 83, 110
Benjamin, Robert D., 116
Benjaminites, 97
Bethlehem, 26, 40–45, 60
betrothal-type scenes, "counter-type
    scene" to, 54
biases, 88–89, 99, 133–34
biblical justice, 17–18
bibliolatry, 135
bitterness, 40, 42
Black Lives Matter movement, 98, 134
Black women, 11–13, 40, 89–90, 133,
    136
    the "StrongBlack (sic) Woman," 12
    *See also* African American women;
        womanist scholarship; women of
        color
blessings, 42, 60–61, 64, 94–95
Boaz, 5
    attitude toward Ruth, 46–47, 57
    as David's great-grandfather, 62
    generosity to Ruth, 46–47, 52, 57
    identity of, 22
    as kinsman/redeemer, 46, 51, 59–63
    marriage to Ruth, 23–24, 28, 35, 43,
        60–63
    motivations of, 57
    as Naomi's (Elimelech's) relative,
        46–47, 51, 59–63
    Ruth's introduction to, 46
    Ruth's nighttime encounter with,
        51–52
    son with Ruth, 43, 63–64, 66
Book of Discipline, 95
Bowen, Nancy R., 3
Buddhism, 2

Burke, Tarana, 82
Butting, Klara, 109
Byron, Gay L., 10–11
bystanders, 111

"Cablinasian" identity, 88n2
Cannon, Katie G., 10
Catholic Church, 95
Chauvin, Derek, 109–10
Cheng, Patrick S., 95
child labor, 31
childlessness, 24, 38, 67
    barrenness, 40, 42
Chilion (Orpah's deceased husband/
    Naomi's son), 26, 28, 42, 59
choices
    ethical, 52, 57
    by oppressed groups, 4
    by persons of color, 40
    reproductive, 83–85
    *See also* survival
*Chosen Exile, A: A History of Racial
    Passing* (Hobbs), 88
Christ. *See* Jesus Christ
Christian canon, 72
Christianity, 120, 123
    the Great Commission, 37
    missionaries, 36–37
    used to enslave, 134
    *See also* Catholic Church; churches;
        Protestant Christianity
churches
    conflict in, 106
    ecclesiology, 120
    as microcosm of society, 93–94
    *See also* leadership; pastors
citizenship, 30–31, 114
city gate, 59, 61–62
civil rights, 78, 117
class, socioeconomic, 49
    classism, 4, 89, 94
    class stratification, 79
Clifton, Lucille, 123
climate change, 33
Cold War era, 30
collaboration, *16*

INDEX OF SUBJECTS

**145**

colonialism, 8–10
colonization, 8–9, 77, 84
comedic structure, 23
common good, 85, 106
community
 covenant, 43, 45, 52
 flourishing, 65
 and "traditional communalism"
  worldview, 55
 *See also* churches
compassion, 38, 111
compliance, 67, 77–78, 97
Concern Worldwide US, 29–30
concubinage, 3, 87, 107–8
confession, 36, 123
conflict, 135–36
 in book of Esther, 74
 in book of Ruth, 24
 church as site of, 106
 Esther as transformative mediator,
  116–17
 ethnic, 97
 generative quality of, 136
 interreligious and intercultural, 14
 intractable, 29, 98–99, 131, 136
 prayer and, 106
 refugees from, 29–30
 religious sanction of, 127
 resolution/transformation of, 15–18,
  27–28, 38–39, 116–17, 122,
  135–36 (*See also* religious ethical
  mediation)
 Ruth as mediator of, 38–39
 spiral of, 102
 trickster myths and, 55
 *See also* violence
conscience, 120
conversion, 43, 56
corruption, 30–31
Cottrill, Amy C., 28, 66
counter-socialization, 41
counter-type scene, 54
courage, moral. *See* moral courage
covenant, Mosaic. *See* Mosaic covenant
COVID-19 pandemic, 98, 102–3
Creation, 6, 32, 67, 99

cultures
 and culturalism, 135
 intercultural conflict, 14
 overlapping, 116
 *See also* deception, culture of; moral
  courage: culture of

Dalit religions, 36
Daniel, book of, 72
David, 12, 21, 60, 63–67
 genealogy of, 45, 64–67
Day, Keri, 80
deception, culture of, 13, 16–17, 24, 56,
  73–74, 116, 126–28
 and "trickster" motif, 54–56, 108,
  116
decrees, 76, 79, 86, 93
 to annihilate the Jews, 97–101
 Mordecai's counter-decree/the Great
  Reversal, 121–24, 126, 130n8
Delilah, 3
dialogue, 14, 23, 34, 136
dignity, 54, 83, 101, 110. *See also*
  *individual names, e.g.,* Vashti
disability
 and ableism, 94
 passing, 88n3
discipleship, xiii, 17, 91
discrimination, 40, 50, 93, 95, 99, 103.
  *See also by description, e.g.,* racism
disobedience. *See* obedience/
  disobedience
displacement, 29–30
diversity, xiv–xv, 22
divine intervention, 74
domination, 6, 16, 75, 105, 118
 and "outsider/within" marginal
  location, 105
Dreifus, Erika, 66
Dube, Musa W., 9–10, 33–34
Dunbar, Ericka Shawndricka, 75

Ecclesiastes, book of, 71
ecclesiology, 120
ego needs, 105–6, 113
8P Freedom Framework, 91

**146** INDEX OF SUBJECTS

elders, 59–61

Elimelech (Naomi's deceased husband), 26–29, 31–32, 36, 59–63

Elkanah, 64

El Shaddai, 22

encounter, tensions of, 16, 18, 22, 24–25, 56, 67

enslavement. *See* slavery

Ephrathah, 60

epistemology, 116

equality, 2–3, 117

Equal Justice Initiative, 98

equity, 18, 79

eschatological hope, 65

Esther, 71–132

  banquets of, 104–5

  beauty of, 86–87

  becoming queen, 74, 86–92, 96

  as counter voice, 71–72

  deception as used by, 108

  as foreigner, 5

  Hadassah as Jewish name of, 72–73

  and Hegai (king's eunuch), 86–87

  "If I perish, I perish," 101, 109

  Jewish identity revealed by, 121

  Jewish people as saved by, 74, 121

  as Jewish woman, 4, 122

  meaning of name, 72

  as moral agent, 73, 106–11

  moral ambiguity of, 108

  moral courage of, 73–74, 116, 126, 133

  Mordecai as saved by, 74

  as Mordecai's adopted daughter (*see* Mordecai)

  obedience of, 87, 107–8

  as offered half the kingdom, 104, 115

  as orphan, 106

  "outsider/within" marginal location, 105

  petition of, 115

  profession of sacrifice, 133

  Purim as established by, 129–30

  as "quadruply disadvantaged individual," 106

  as religious ethical mediator, 18

  as role model, 136

  survival choices made by, 13

  as transformative mediator, 116–17

Esther, book of, 71–132

  ethnic conflict in, 97

  four major plot moves in, 74

  as historical fiction, 72

  importance to Jewish tradition, 130

  as novella, 72–73

  as parody and comedy, 130

  reading through hermeneutics of religious ethical mediation, 73–74, 79–85, 87–95, 97–99, 101–3, 105–6, 116–20, 122–24, 126–28, 130–32

  reversals in, 121–24

"The Esther Narratives as Reminders— for Jews and for Christians" (Bachmann), 130

ethics

  and ethical choices, 52, 57

  and finding ethical responses, 6, 15–17, 135

  law and, 74, 128

  and means-end thinking, 117

  womanist ethical interpretation, xvii, 10, 15, 80, 120, 134–36

  *See also* religious ethical mediation

ethnicity, xv, 2–4, 13–14, 40, 49

  Esther as mediator and, 116

  and ethnic cleansing, 6

  and ethnic conflict, 97

  and hate crimes, 71

  and interethnic tension, 57

  multiethnicity, 88

  and racial/ethnic inclusiveness, 65, 94

  of Ruth, 44–45, 48, 66

  and violence, 73

  *See also* race; *specific topics, e.g.,* passing

ethnocentrism, 6, 118

eunuchs, 76, 86–87, 100–101, 113, 115

  murder plot by, 92–95

  *See also* Hathach; Hegai

Europe, 29

INDEX OF SUBJECTS

147

evangelicals, white, 81–82
excess, 128
exclusion, 35–36
   violence of, 66
exclusivism, 22–23
exile, 21, 73, 86, 88, 106
exploitation
   economic, 31
   sexual, 71, 90–91
extremism
   progressive, 41
   religious, 29

faithfulness. *See* hesed
"fake news" accusation, 80
family
   Boaz as kinsman/redeemer, 46, 51,
      59–63
   loyalty to, 24, 38 (*See also under
      individual names, e.g.,* Naomi:
      Ruth's loyalty to)
   *See also* genealogy; kinship
famine, 5, 26–33, 56–57, 60
fasting, 100, 104
"father's house," 22n6, 27
femininity, 89
feminist scholarship, 6–7, 14, 22, 32,
      34–35, 41, 44, 49, 53, 78, 81
   and feminist hermeneutics, 7
   *See also* womanist scholarship;
      *individual names*
Fentress-Williams, Judy, 22–23, 27,
      41–42
festivals, 122, 130. *See also* banquets;
      Purim
Fishman, Sylvia Barack, 106
five scrolls (Megilloth), 71
flourishing, human, 65, 111
Floyd, George, 109–10
folktale, Northern Sotho, 108
food insecurity, 6, 28–29
foreignness, 5, 21, 33
   of Esther, 5
   of Ruth, 5, 12, 23–24, 27, 31, 33–34,
      38–39, 43–46, 48–49, 54–56, 62,
      67
   *See also* "Others"; strangers

foreign wives, 5, 21, 34, 62. *See also*
      intermarriage
forgiveness, 36, 53, 82, 123
Francis, Pope, 95
Frazier, Darnella, 109–10
Freedom Prayer, 91–92
friendship, 2, 27, 35, 37

Gafney, Wilda, 11, 38n
gate, city (Boaz at), 59, 61–62
gate, king's, 92–93, 104
gender discrimination, 50
gender-exclusive language, 89
gender expectations, 57
gender identity, 88–89, 94–95
gender justice, 41, 45
gender oppression, 4
genealogy, 5
   of David, 45, 64–67
   female, 23
generations
   and intergenerational tension, 57
   *See also* genealogy
generosity, 47, 57
genocide, 84, 97, 105, 122
Gentiles, 72
*Gleaners, The* (painting by Millet), 48
gleaning, 28, 46–49, 57
Gnanadason, Aruna, 36, 38
God, 17
   actions of, 32, 63
   and divine intervention, 74
   El Shaddai, 22
   *hesed* (faithfulness) of, 16, 18, 24–25,
      67
   "hidden," 74
   image of, 18, 132
   Jewish relationship to, 130
   justice of, 13–14, 16–18, 23–24, 37,
      73–74, 79, 83–85, 111, 132
   Naomi's, 22, 34, 42, 58
   nature of, 71
   presence of, 73–74
   providence of, 73–74
   will of, 128

**148**  INDEX OF SUBJECTS

God (*continued*)
    YHWH, 41, 45
    *See also* Mosaic covenant
gods, Moabite, 34n14, 41–44
golden scepter, 101, 104, 121
good/goodness
    the common good, 85
    highest, 127
    moral, 84–85
    *See also* ethics
grace, 111
Great Commission, 37
Great Reversal, 121–24, 126, 130n8
gun violence, 1, 135

Hadassah (Esther's Jewish name), 72–73
Hagar, 12–13
halakah, 62
half the kingdom, offer of, 104, 115
Haman
    as Agagite, 96–97
    downfall of, 115–20
    at Esther's banquets, 104–5
    execution of, 115–16
    and the Great Reversal, 121–24, 126,
        130n8
    made to honor Mordecai, 112–13
    Mordecai's animosity with, 97
    Mordecai's refusal to rise for/bow
        before, 104–5
    plot against Mordecai, 104–11
    plot against the Jews, 96–99
    pride and plot of, 104–11
    sons of, 117, 125
    Zeresh as wife of, 104
Hamer, Fannie Lou, 78
Hammedatha the Agagite (father of
    Haman), 96–97
Hannah, 3, 64
hare as trickster, 108
harvests, 47. *See also* barley/barley
    harvest; gleaning
hate crimes, 1, 4, 71, 98
hate speech, 1
Hathach (king's eunuch), 100–101
Hebrew Bible, 35, 54–55, 71, 97, 107

Hegai (king's eunuch), 86–87
*hesed* (faithfulness), 23–24, 39
    God's, 16, 18, 24–25, 67
    risk-taking of, 24–25, 39–40, 64, 67
    *See also under individual names, e.g.,*
        Ruth
heteropatriarchy, 35, 94, 111, 134
heterosexism, 83, 89, 94
"hidden God," 74
hierarchies, 4–5, 16, 87, 89
    hierarchal model of leadership, 94
Hinduism, 2
historical-critical approaches, xiii, 8
Hobbs, Allyson, 88
Holy Spirit, 94, 99, 106
homosexuality, 89–90, 95. *See also entries*
    *beginning with* LGBTQIA+
hope, eschatological, 65
hospitality, 26, 31–32, 47, 57, 75–76
"Hottentot Venus," 77
*Human Flow* (Weiwei), 30
human rights, 29, 84, 90
human trafficking, 3, 6, 90–92
hunger, 28–29
Hurricane Katrina, 30–31

identity, 41–45. *See also under individual*
    *names*
image of God, 18, 132
imagination, moral. *See* moral
    imagination
immigrants, 26–31, 41
    migrant workers, 56
    refugee, 29–31
imperialism, 4, 8–9, 36, 118, 135
incest prohibitions, 62
inclusion, 37, 42, 45, 61, 64, 79, 93–95
India/Indian narratives, 36, 38
inheritance, 36, 59–61
injustice, systemic, 118, 120
integrity, 45
intermarriage, 5, 21, 26, 28, 34, 37–38,
    41–42, 62
intersectionality, 134
    Esther as "quadruply disadvantaged
        individual," 106

# INDEX OF SUBJECTS

Isasi-Días, Ada María, 111
Ishtar, 72
Islam, 2
    Islamophobia, 126
Israel, ancient
    disobedience of, 27, 32
    famine in, 27, 32
    Matriarchs of, 64
    Moab/Moabites, relationship
        with (*see under* Moab, land of/
        Moabites)
Israel, contemporary, 29, 56
    Palestinian-Israeli conflict, 98, 126
Israelite law, 34, 48–49, 54, 127

Japanese Americans, 98
Jephthah's daughter, 3
Jesse, 63
Jesus Christ, 120, 123
Jewish people
    covenantal paradigm of, 130
    decree to annihilate, 97–101
    exiled, 21, 73, 86, 88, 106
    Haman's plot against, 96–99
    mass killing of enemies of, 125–28
    and Mordecai's counter-decree/the
        Great Reversal, 121–24, 126,
        130n8
    relationship to God, 130
    survival of/Esther as saving, 71, 74,
        109, 121, 130, 132
    *See also* Esther; Israel, ancient;
        Judaism; Mordecai
Jobes, Karen H., 74
Johnston, Albert, 88
joy, 65, 130
Judah (ancestor of David), 60
Judah (land), 26, 33, 56–57, 61, 72
Judaism, 2
    and anti-Semitism, 73, 89, 116
    and Purim, 129–30
    *See also* Jewish people
Judges, time of, 21, 32, 64
justice, 18
    agents of, 18
    biblical, 17–18

distributive, 18
Equal Justice Initiative, 98
God's, 13–14, 16–18, 23–24, 37,
    73–74, 79, 83–85, 111, 132
law vs., 73, 116
reparational, 36
reproductive, 50, 83–85
restorative, 16, 67
sexual-gender, 41, 45
social, 84, 136
theocentric, 79
variable definitions of, 123
for women, 83

Katrina, Hurricane, 30–31
Kavanaugh, Brett, 80
Kim, Nadia, 103
kindness, 39. *See also* generosity; *hesed*
King, Martin Luther, Jr., 117
king of Persia. *See* Ahasuerus, King
kinship, 44
    kinsman/redeemer, 46, 51, 59–63
    and levirate marriage, 28, 42, 49, 54,
        60–63
    next-of-kin, 53–54, 59, 62
    *See also* family
Knight, Douglas, 72
Kwok, Pui-lan, 9

land, redemption of. *See* levirate marriage
language
    gender-exclusive, 89
    hate speech, 1
    racist comments, 99
Lapsley, Jacqueline, 42–43
law, 3
    in book of Esther, 128
    ethics and, 74, 128
    vs. justice, 73, 116
    *See also* decrees; Israelite law; Mosaic
        covenant
leadership
    hierarchal model of, 94
    and leader-follower relationship,
        113–14
    and loyalty, 113–14

**150** INDEX OF SUBJECTS

leadership (*continued*)
  public, 113–14
  and relational/shared power, 94, 106
  triangulation of, 113
Leah, 60, 64
Lee, Eunny P., 43–44
lesbian scholarship/interpretation, 35–37
Levine, Amy-Jill, 22n6, 72
levirate law, 5
levirate marriage, 28, 42, 49, 54, 60–63
Levite's concubine, 3
LGBTQIA+
  community, 94
  identity, 91
  rights, 94
liberation, 7
  survival on the way to, 13, 88
liberation theology, 91, 120
lion, 108
literalism, 135
lots, 129–30
love, radical, 95
Lovelace, Vanessa, 10–11
loyalty, 38, 64
  and leader-follower relationship, 113–14
  *See also hesed; individual names*
*Lynched: The Power of Memory in a Culture of Terror* (Sims), 120
lynching, 98, 118, 120

Maathai, Wangari, 33
Mahlon (Ruth's deceased husband/ Naomi's son), 26, 28, 42, 43, 59
Malawi, 56
Malcolm X, 117–18
Mandela, Nelson, 77
manipulation, 54, 105–6
  and "subversive acquiescence," 55
  *See also* deception, culture of; seduction; "trickster" motif
Mara, Naomi's name change to, 40, 42
marginalization/the marginalized, 2, 6, 14, 24, 37, 41, 55, 64–66, 90, 95
  and Esther's "outsider/within" location, 105
  *See also* "Others"

marriage
  abduction or rape-marriage, 38n
  levirate, 28, 42, 49, 54, 60–63
  of Ruth and Boaz, 23–24, 28, 35, 43, 60–64
  same-sex, 95
Martin, Clarice, 11
masculinity, 75, 89
Masenya, Madipoane (Ngwan'a Mphahlele), 35n18, 108
mass killing, 102, 118, 121, 125–26, 128, 135. *See also* genocide
Matriarchs of Israel, 64
matriarchy, 89–90
McTernan, Oliver, 2
means-end thinking, 117
mediation, transformative, 16–17, 24, 38, 55, 67, 73, 109, 116, 126, 135. *See also* religious ethical mediation
Megilloth (five scrolls), 71
men
  authority of, king's decree on, 76, 79, 86
  and masculinity, 75, 89
  *See also* patriarchy
metaphors, 3, 107
#MeToo movement, 82–83
Middle East conflict, 29, 98, 126
migrant workers, 56
Milano, Alyssa, 82
Millet, Jean-Francois, 48
misogyny, 7
missionaries, 36–37
Mississippi, 78
Moab, land of/Moabites, 26–29, 33, 38, 41–42, 43–44, 61. *See also under* Ruth: as Moabite
"model minority," 103
monarchial and patriarchal, 75–76, 132
moral agency/moral agents, 4, 14–18, 24, 56, 126, 136
  Esther as moral agent, 73, 106–11
  Naomi as moral agent, 67
  Ruth as moral agent, 24–25, 38–39, 56, 67
  Vashti as moral agent, 76–79

# INDEX OF SUBJECTS

moral ambiguity, 108, 116
moral courage, 13, 16–17, 24, 56, 116
    culture of, 16, 38–39, 116
    of Esther, 73–74, 116, 126, 133
    of Ruth, 24, 38–39, 67
    of Vashti, 77, 79
moral imagination, 16, 24, 38–39, 67, 73
Mordecai
    as Benjaminite, 97
    counter-decree of/the Great
        Reversal, 121–24, 126, 130n8
    disobedience/insubordination of, 101
    Esther as adopted daughter of, 86
    Esther as saving, 74
    Haman as forced to honor, 112–13
    Haman's animosity with, 97
    Haman's plot against, 104–11
    lament of, 100
    patriarchal power of, 132
    promotion of, 132
    refusal to rise for/bow before
        Haman, 104–5
    as saving the king, 74, 112
    *See also* Jewish people
Mosaic covenant, 28, 42–43
    and covenant community, 43, 45, 52
    and covenantal obligations, 57
    disobedience to, 32
    paradigm of Jewish relationship to
        God, 130
motherhood, 13. *See also* childlessness;
    reproductive justice; surrogacy
"mother's house," 22, 27, 33–34
mothers-in-law, 53. *See also under*
    Naomi: as mother-in-law
mujerista theology, 111
multiethnicity, 88, 97
multinational corporations, 31
multiracialism, 84, 88
music, 35, 50
Muslims. *See* Islam
myths, 40, 55, 89, 103, 128

Nadar, Sarojini, 44, 53–54
Naomi
    attitudes toward Ruth, 56–57

    Boaz as kinsman of, 46–47, 51,
        59–63
    as estranged woman, 58
    God of, 22, 34, 41, 58
    identity of, 22, 41–43
    as moral agent, 67
    as mother-in-law, 13, 22, 26–27, 33,
        43–44, 47, 51–53, 57, 63
    name change to Mara, 40, 42
    privilege of, 43
    Ruth as better than "seven sons" to,
        63
    Ruth as surrogate for, 61–62, 66
    Ruth's loyalty to, 24, 39, 43–45, 57,
        63, 67
    sons of, deceased, 26, 28, 42, 44, 59
    as widow, 34, 42, 49, 54 (*See also*
        Elimelech)
nationalism, 6
neighbor, 41
Newsom, Carol A., 7
Niebuhr, H. Richard, 120
nonviolence, 33
    and nonviolent resistance, 135
normativity/normative views
    and beauty standards, 49–50
    challenges to, 71–72
Northern Sotho folktale, 108
Norton, Yolanda, 37, 54–55

Obama, Michelle, 50
Obed (son of Ruth and Boaz), 63, 66
obedience/disobedience, 27, 32, 53, 87,
    89, 101, 107–8
O'Connor, Kathleen, 7
Old Testament, 27, 32, 34–35
    Megilloth (five scrolls), 71
    scholarship, 7, 11, 22, 49, 108
    *See also* Hebrew Bible
omnipresence of God's hesed, 67
omnipresence of God's justice, 14,
    16–17, 23–24, 37, 73, 83
omnipresence of violence, 2, 5–6, 14–17,
    24, 67, 73, 126, 132
    complicity in, 135–36
    the term, 134

oppression
and choices, 4
complicity with, 45
gender, 4, 6–7, 9, 40–41
resistance to, 74, 76, 116
and sacrificing another oppressed
group, 93
systems of, 89, 93
and worldview of oppressors, 87–88
*See also by description, e.g.,*
colonialism; patriarchy
Organization of Afro-American Unity,
117
Orpah, 26, 33–34, 38, 42, 77
deceased husband of (*see* Chilion)
orphans, 62
Esther as, 106
"Others"/otherness/othering, 2, 4, 15,
23, 40, 43, 49, 57, 134. *See also*
foreignness; strangers
"outsider/within" marginal location, 105

Palestinian-Israeli conflict, 98, 126
parables, reading Esther and Ruth as,
71–72
partisan polarization, 113–14
passing, 87–89, 93, 122
pastors, 80, 82, 93–94, 106. *See also*
leadership
patriarchs, Old Testament, 27
patriarchy, 4–5, 9–10, 23, 26, 34, 47,
54, 64, 66, 73–85, 102–3, 106,
134–35
heteropatriarchy, 35, 94, 111, 134
monarchial and patriarchal power,
75–76, 132
power and privilege of, 73–83, 87,
89, 97, 111, 116
white supremacist, 80, 103
women's access to privilege of, 89
Peninnah, 3
Pentecostal churches, 35n18
Perez (Tamar's son), 60, 64
persecution, 4, 6, 29–30
Persia, king of. *See* Ahasuerus, King
Persian Empire
king of (*see* Ahasuerus, King)

Susa as capital of (*see* Susa, city of)
*See also* Esther, book of; *individual
names, e.g.,* Haman
Persian period, 72
persons of color, 39–40. *See also* women
of color
Peters, Rebecca Todd, 84–85
plagues, 27, 92
the COVID-19 pandemic, 98, 102–3
pluralism, 22
poetry, 123
*Postcolonial Feminist Interpretation of the
Bible* (Dube), 9–10
postcolonial scholarship, 6, 8–10,
14, 33–34, 36, 56, 84. *See also
individual names*
postexilic period, 21
poverty/the poor, 6, 28, 48–49, 62, 111,
129
power
monarchial and patriarchal, 75–76,
94, 132
relational/shared, 94, 106
structures of, 78–79, 82, 93, 97, 113
*See also by description, e.g.,* patriarchy;
leadership
praxis, 91, 111
prayer, 83, 91, 106, 132
Freedom Prayer, 91–92
for marriage of Boaz and Ruth, 60–61
prejudices, 88–89
pride, Haman's, 104–11
privilege, 43, 73–74, 79–81, 87, 89, 111,
116
procreation, 50. *See also* childlessness;
motherhood; reproductive justice
progressive extremism, 41
pro-life stance, 82, 85
Protestant Christianity, xiv, 95
white evangelicals, 81–82
*See also specific denominations*
providence, divine, 73–74
Pui-lan, Kwok, 9
Purim, Feast of, 129–30

quality of life, 12–14, 23
queens. *See under* Esther; Vashti

## INDEX OF SUBJECTS

race, 49
  and beauty norms, 49–50
  Black-white racial binary, 103
  multiracialism, 84, 88
  race relations, 98
  and racial/ethnic inclusiveness, 65,
    94
  racial terror, 98
  *See also by description;* ethnicity;
    racism; *specific topics, e.g.,* passing
Rachel, 60, 64
Racial Justice Center, 119
racism, 4, 9, 50, 89, 99, 103, 117. *See also*
    white supremacy
radical love, 95
rape, 81
  #MeToo movement, 82–83
  rape-marriage, 38n
  rape shield laws, 50
Ray, Stephen, 89–90
rebellion, 10, 102
reconciliation, 14, 17, 24, 67
redemption, 61, 67, 74, 111
  Boaz as redeemer, 46, 51, 59–63
redemption of land. *See* levirate marriage
refugees, 29–31
relational/shared power, 94, 106
religion
  and interreligious conflict/religious
    sanction of conflict, 14, 127
  and interreligious tension, 57
  Moabite, 34n14, 41–44
  Naomi's God, 22, 34, 41, 58
  and religious violence, 29, 73
  *See also specific religions, e.g.,*
    Christianity; Judaism; *specific
    topics, e.g.,* passing
Religious Community for Reproductive
    Choice (RCRC), 84
religious ethical mediation, 15–18, 79,
    133–36
  by Esther, 16
  Great Commission as practice of, 37
  and moral agency, 16 (*See also* moral
    agency)
  practicing, 106

reading Esther through hermeneutics
  of, 73–74, 79–85, 87–95, 97–99,
  101–3, 105–6, 116–20, 122–24,
  126–28, 130–32
reading Ruth through hermeneutics
  of, 24–25, 28–33, 38–41, 44–45,
  47, 49–50, 52–58, 60–61, 65–67
  by Ruth, 16, 38–39
  a womanist hermeneutics of, 16–17,
  23, 67
  *See also* transformative mediation
religious violence, 2, 73, 127
reparational justice, 36
reproductive justice, 50, 83–85
reputation, 78
resistance, 74, 76, 116
  female, 76–85
  nonviolent, 135
restorative justice, 16, 67
revenge, 97, 122–23
reversals, 128
  the Great Reversal, 121–24, 126,
  130n8
Ringe, Sharon H., 7
risk-taking, 24–25, 39–40, 64, 67
ritual theory, 107–8
*Roe v. Wade,* 50, 83
role models, 7, 12, 35, 133, 136
Rowland, Dick, 119
Russell, Letty, 32
Ruth, 21–67
  beauty and youth of, 48, 56
  as better than "seven sons," 63
  Boaz's attitude toward, 57
  Boaz's generosity to, 47, 52, 57
  Boaz's introduction to, 46
  boldness of, 54
  as counter voice, 71–72
  as daughter-in-law, 13, 22, 26–27, 33,
    43–45, 47, 51–53, 57, 63
  as David's great-grandmother, 62
  dignity of, 54
  ethnicity of, 44–45, 48, 66
  foreignness of, 5, 12, 23–24, 27, 31,
    33–34, 38–39, 43–46, 48–49,
    54–56, 62, 67

**154**  INDEX OF SUBJECTS

Ruth (*continued*)
    gleaning in the fields, 28, 46–49, 57
    *hesed* (faithfulness) of, 24, 39, 43–45,
        57, 61, 63–64, 67, 133
    hybridity of, 43–44
    identity of, 22, 43–45, 66
    as immigrant, 26–31, 41
    as initiator of relationships, 57
    integrity of, 45
    marriage to Boaz, 23–24, 28, 35, 43,
        60–64
    as migrant worker, 56
    as Moabite, 4, 21, 23, 26–29, 33–34,
        37–38, 41–46, 48, 55, 59–61, 64,
        66
    as moral agent, 24–25, 38–39, 56, 67
    moral courage of, 24, 38–39, 67
    Naomi's attitudes toward, 56–57
    as Naomi's surrogate, 61–62, 66
    nighttime encounter with Boaz,
        51–52
    as religious ethical mediator, 18,
        38–39
    as role model, 136
    son of, 43, 63–64, 66
    as subversive character, 44
    survival, choices regarding, 13
    as transformative religious ethical
        mediator, 38–39
    vow of, 33–35, 37–39, 41–43, 45, 57,
        61, 67, 133
    as widow, 12, 27–28, 34, 42, 43, 49,
        54, 62 (*See also* Mahlon)
    as "woman of valor," 43
Ruth, book of, 21–62, 71–72, 74
    author of, 22, 28
    comedic structure to, 23
    dialogical reading of, 23
    reading through hermeneutics of
        religious ethical mediation,
        24–25, 28–33, 38–41, 44–45, 47,
        49–50, 52–58, 60–61, 65–67

sackcloth and ashes, 100
sacrifice, 136
    of another oppressed group, 93
    Esther's profession of, 133

Sakenfeld, Katharine Doob, 22, 39, 49,
    65
salvation, 91–92, 111, 127, 130
same-sex civil unions, 95
same-sex marriage, 95
Samson, 3
sandal ceremony, 59, 61–62
Sarah, 64
#SayHerName movement, 134
scapegoating, 31, 102
scepter, golden, 101, 104, 121
Second Amendment to US Constitution,
    135
seduction, 47, 53–54
self-control, 107
self-defense, 117–18, 122, 126
September 11, 2001, 120, 123, 126
seven eunuchs, 76, 93
"seven sons," 63
sexism, 4, 7, 9, 109
    heterosexism, 83, 89, 94
sex trafficking, 90. *See also* human
    trafficking
sexual abuse, 82–83
sexual exploitation, 71, 90–91
sexual-gender justice, 41, 45
sexual harassment, 50, 80–83
sexuality, 47, 95
sexual violence, 3, 82–83. *See also* rape
Sharapova, Maria, 50
Sheppard, Phillis, 131
signet ring, 96, 121–22
Sikhism, 2
silence, 2–3, 40, 66, 82–83, 101, 134
#SilenceIsNotSpiritual campaign, 82–83
Sims, Angela D., 120
singleness, 49
sin-talk, 89–90, 111
Siquans, Agnethe, 62
SisterSong—Women of Color
    Reproductive Justice (RJ)
    Collective, 84
six measures of barley, 51–52
slavery, 12, 77, 80, 84, 115, 127, 134
Smith, Mitzi J., xvii, 11, 13–14
snake, 108
social justice, 84, 136

INDEX OF SUBJECTS

solidarity, 14, *16*, 30–32, 35–36, 44–45, 73–74, 82, 111, 116
"soteriological praxis for bystanders," 111
South Africa, 35n18, 77
speech. *See* language
Spirit, Holy. *See* Holy Spirit
steadfastness. *See* hesed
stereotypes, 40, 89, 103
stewardship, 32
"The Story of Ruth, in Three Poems" (Dreifus), 66
storytelling, 9–10, 22, 35, 55
strangers, 26, 32, 35–36, 41, 71. *See also* foreignness; "Others"
"StrongBlack (sic) Woman," 12
"subversive acquiescence," 55
Sugirtharajah, R. S., 8
Supreme Court, US
    Kavanaugh hearings, 80
    *Roe v. Wade,* 50, 83
surrogacy, 13
    of Ruth, 61–62, 66
survival, 23–26, 31–34, 39, 49–55, 109
    actions necessary for, 87–88
    competitive, 93–94
    in exile, 73
    individual and communal, 133
    Jewish, 71, 74, 109, 121, 130, 132
    passing as strategy for, 87–89, 93, 122
    and quality of life, 12–15, 73
    Ruth and Esther as stories of, 71
    seduction as strategy for, 47
    of the small and powerless, 108
    on the way to liberation, 13, 88
Susa, city of, 75, 97, 100–101, 109, 117, 121–22, 125, 129

Tamar, 3, 60, 64
Taylor, Breonna, 78
tensions, 57. *See also* encounter, tensions of
terror, racial, 98
Thistlethwaite, Susan Brooks, 81
Title IX of the Education Amendments, 50
Torah, 62
"traditional communalism," 55

tragedies, reversal of. *See* reversals
transformative mediation, 16–17, 24, 38, 67, 73, 109, 116, 126, 135
    trickster myth and, 55
    *See also* religious ethical mediation
trauma, 80
    collective, 131
triangulation, 113
"trickster" motif, 54–56, 108, 116
Trump, Donald, 80–82, 102, 113–14
truth/truthfulness, 116
Tulsa Race Massacre, 118–19

UNHCR (United Nations High Commissioner of Refugees), 29
United Methodist denomination, 95
United Nations Entity for Gender Equality and Empowerment for Women, 2–3
United Nations High Commissioner of Refugees (UNHCR), 29
United Nations international human rights framework, 84
United States
    race relations in, 98
    September 11, 2001, 120, 123, 126
    *See also individual names; specific topics and events*

Vashti, Queen, 74–79, 82, 87, 93, 101–2, 105–7, 109
    banishment of, 74
    as moral agent, 76–79
    moral courage of, 77, 79
Vasko, Elisabeth T., 110–11
violence, 15–16
    ethical responses to, 17–18
    ethnic/religious, 2, 29, 73, 127
    of exclusion, 66
    gendered, 2–5, 14–18, 23–24, 26, 28, 34, 36, 38–41, 45, 47, 49, 66–67, 73, 79, 89, 133–34
    metaphorical, 3
    moral agency and, 136
    nature of, 4–5
    omnipresence of (*see* omnipresence of violence)

violence (*continued*)
    refugees from, 29–30
    resisting, 111, 135
    retaliatory, 122–23
    sexual, 3, 82–83
    spiral of, 118
    state-sanctioned, 119, 133
    systems of, 4
    women and, 3–6
    *See also* nonviolence; omnipresence
        of violence; self-defense
virgins, 86, 90, 107, 128
voter suppression, 81
voting rights, 78, 81–82
vow, Ruth's. *See under* Ruth: vow of

wages, 31
Walker, Alice, 10
Walker-Barnes, Chanequa, 12
Weems, Renita J., 11–12
weeping, 65, 100
Weinstein, Harvey, 82
Weiwei, Ai, 30
wheat harvest, 47
whiteness, and beauty norms, 50
white supremacy, 80, 94, 103, 111, 120,
    134–35. *See also* racism
widows/widowhood, 12, 62. *See also* by
    name, e.g., Naomi; Ruth
Williams, Delores, 11–13
Williams, Serena, 50
witnesses, 59–60, 72
womanist scholarship/interpretation, 6,
    10–18, 23, 37, 53–55, 66–67, 80,
    120, 131, 133–36
    hermeneutical presuppositions of,
        15–18, 23
    womanist ethical interpretation, xvii,
        10, 15, 80, 120, 134–36
    *See also individual names/scholars*

women, 4
    and access to patriarchal privilege, 89
    and complicity with oppression, 45
    and female worldviews, 22–23
    and femininity, 89
    friendship between, 2, 27, 35, 37
    justice for, 83
    norms for, 71
    as property, 47
    as social group, 4, 79, 83, 89
    *See also by name; specific topics and
        descriptions, e.g.,* Black women;
        widows
women of color, 13, 39–40, 49–50, 84,
    133–34. *See also* Black women;
    womanist scholarship
*Women's Bible Commentary, The*
    (Newsom and Ringe, eds.), 7
Women's Day services, 133
Woods, Tiger, 88n2
worldviews, 11, 87
    colonial, 10
    female, 22–23
    of oppressors, 87–88
    of "traditional communalism," 55
    Trump rallies as performance of,
        113–14
World War II, 88, 98
worship, 41–42, 83, 91, 135

X, Malcolm, 117–18
xenophobia, 29, 74

Yee, Gale A., 27, 43, 49, 87
YHWH, 41, 45
Young, Anjanette, 77–78

Zeresh (wife of Haman), 104

www.ingramcontent.com/pod-product-compliance
Lightning Source LLC
Chambersburg PA
CBHW022008030425
24573CB00001B/1